# ISRAEL UNDER FIRE

## JOHN ANKERBERG
## JIMMY DeYOUNG
### WITH DILLON BURROUGHS

HARVEST HOUSE PUBLISHERS

EUGENE, OREGON

*Cover by Dugan Design Group, Bloomington, Minnesota*

**ISRAEL UNDER FIRE**
Copyright © 2009 by The John Ankerberg Theological Research Institute and Jimmy DeYoung
Published by Harvest House Publishers
Eugene, Oregon 97402
www.harvesthousepublishers.com

Library of Congress Cataloging-in-Publication Data
Ankerberg, John, 1945-
    Israel under fire / John Ankerberg and Jimmy DeYoung, with Dillon Burroughs.
      p. cm.
    Includes bibliographical references.
    ISBN 978-0-7369-2584-6 (pbk.)
    1. Bible—Prophecies—Israel. 2. Israel. 3. Bible—Prophecies. I. DeYoung, Jimmy. II. Burroughs, Dillon.
III. Title.
    BS649.P3A55 2009
    236.'9—dc22

                                                                                    2009017208

# CONTENTS

**Part Four: Investigating Israel in the Book of Revelation**

I s Israel really under fire? President Mahmoud Ahmadinejad of Iran has vowed to "wipe Israel off the map." Pope Benedict's 2009 visit of Israel called for the establishment of a Palestinian state that would divide the land of Israel. Rockets continue to enter the borders of Israel from Hezbollah in the north and Hamas in the south. Israel is *literally* under fire.

Yet in addition to the military and terrorist conflicts aimed toward the land of Abraham, Isaac, and Jacob, we find ancient Bible prophecies nearing their fulfillment. Ezekiel 38 and 39 speak of a coming war that I believe will occur just prior to the Tribulation period in which Russia and many Middle Eastern nations will align against Israel. The Bible also predicts the nations of the world (possibly including even the United States) will abandon Israel, leaving the nation for God alone to rescue through His supernatural power.

To the surprise of many, today's political, military, and academic leaders have made statements that echo the prophets of old. In *Israel Under Fire,* Dr. John Ankerberg and Dr. Jimmy DeYoung take us directly into the presence of these key influencers. From Israeli Prime Minister Benjamin Netanyahu, Knesset speaker Reuven Rivlin, retired U.S. General Jerry Boykin, and many others we hear how today's politics increasingly interact with the predictions made long ago in God's Word.

Any person serious about knowing how current news connects with biblical prophecy will appreciate the research in *Israel Under Fire*. Written by scholars of both Scripture and media, you'll find an approach that honors God and seeks to learn from the events taking place in our world today.

In the end, those who read this book's pages will walk away with a new appreciation for the prophecies of God's Word, eager to live the message of Christ until His return.

—Dr. Tim LaHaye, bestselling coauthor
of the Left Behind® series and founder of
the Pre-Trib Research Center

# WHY SHOULD WE CARE ABOUT ISRAEL'S FUTURE?

*"We're not only being told that we'll be wiped off the face of the earth, but also that Iranian-backed proxies are establishing themselves at our doorsteps and rocketing our people."*

—BENJAMIN NETANYAHU, PRIME MINISTER OF ISRAEL

*"If no one will take [action] and Israel will have to take [action] on our own, we will have to consider and evaluate what we have to do."*

—REUVEN RIVLIN, ISRAEL'S SPEAKER OF THE KNESSET

*"I agree with those Israelis that have told you they fear Iran as their number one threat. I think that it is. I think Iran is the number one threat probably to the whole world."*

—RETIRED U.S. LIEUTENANT GENERAL JERRY BOYKIN

*"Nuclear capability in the hands of the Iranians is not only a threat against Israel, it is a threat to the whole world."*

—MOSHE ARENS, FORMER ISRAELI MINISTER OF DEFENSE

Today, the modern State of Israel stands as a monument to fulfilled biblical prophecy. As Israel's first prime minister, David Ben-Gurion stated, "If you know the history, the modern story of

Israel, if you know the story of Israel and what happened here, and you do not believe in miracles, you are not realistic. Something is wrong with you."[1]

Together, we sought to speak directly with key leaders of the nation of Israel and some of its surrounding nations to experience these monumental historical events firsthand. I (Jimmy) have lived in Jerusalem since 1991. God has provided opportunities throughout my years in the Middle East to interview every Israeli prime minister over the last 18 years, as well as Jordan's King Abdullah, and the late Palestinian leader Yasser Arafat.

When John and I first began to discuss the concept of traveling together in the land of Israel to interview leaders on this issue of Israel under fire, it was quickly evident that a unique partnership was taking place.

First, John has invested his life in interviewing experts to provide vital information about Christianity to those interested in learning more. Second, we share a similar passion for helping people understand how God's Word, including its prophecies, impact our lives today. Between the two of us, there was plenty of experience as well as a passion to understand and communicate God's work in the modern nation of Israel.

In April 2008, we embarked on a 17-day journey to interview many of the top political, military, and spiritual leaders of the nation of Israel as they marked their sixtieth anniversary as a modern nation. What we experienced was an amazing story.

One clear theme woven throughout all of our interviews was the idea that the warnings from Israel's political leaders about future issues frequently echoed the statements made by Jewish prophets from thousands of years ago. Without exception, each expert we met provided remarks that fit the puzzle of often mysterious passages of Bible prophecy.

As we returned home to sort through the 70-plus hours of footage and 700 pages of transcripts we had gathered, we observed two clear and compelling concepts. First, Israel's historical story is an incredible series of events pointing toward the supernatural intervention of a sovereign God. Second, Israel is under fire both politically and militarily. The issues confronting Israel's leaders today are vital in terms of both world politics *and* prophetic importance, because God has spoken about the events taking place in Israel now and those that will unfold in the days ahead.

We hope as you join us in recounting and researching these events that you'll experience for yourself how God is at work in the *land* of Israel and among the *people* of Israel. In addition, we believe you'll see numerous connections between the contemporary challenges to Israel with the clear and urgent predictions given through the pages of God's Word generations ago.

Our goal is not to simply share information with you, though there is much to be learned. We ultimately desire for you to connect with the struggles and joys of the Jewish people in a way that helps you experience the sense of urgency facing the nation—and our world— today. These issues will not only impact our daily lives, but our world's destiny.

PART ONE

# ISRAEL'S PROPHETIC DESTINY

# Chapter 1

# A People Regathered

W e were in Jerusalem prior to the May 2008 sixtieth anniversary celebration of the modern nation of Israel. Many have lauded this milestone as a monument to the fulfillment of biblical prophecy. We wanted to find out why. As we talked to those in the government, the military, the Jewish settlements, and religious leaders, we quickly discovered why. We traveled to the thriving modern city of Tel Aviv along the Mediterranean Sea to Independence Hall, where it all started in 1948 when David Ben-Gurion, surrounded by just a handful of Jewish leaders, stunned the world by announcing the reformed nation of Israel.

As we entered the historic and much-photographed building, we interviewed Itzik Dror, director of Independence Hall and an expert on modern Israeli history. We began by asking him the obvious: "What did the important events that took place in this building sixty years ago mean to the Jewish people?"

As he brought us through the doors into the different rooms, Dror answered in his thick Hebrew accent, "This building is a historic building because Israel was born here. And this was one of the greatest moments in the history of our people."

His response would later find itself reiterated through the voice of an expert more well-known in the United States—retired Lieutenant

General William G. Boykin (also called "Jerry Boykin"). Boykin served as the U.S. deputy undersecretary of defense for intelligence and as an expert in international counterterrorism. He was in Jerusalem during the taping of our documentary and graciously agreed to do an interview. His answers proved extremely insightful on the issues confronting the modern nation of Israel.

Boykin shared, "I think the very fact that the nation of Israel was reestablished sixty years ago, the very fact that it has gone from probably in 1948 [from] less than a half million Jews to a country of almost seven million now, is all prophecy being fulfilled. The Jews are being regathered to the land of Israel."

In the Jewish community of Hebron, the land where Abraham once walked and received the promises from God about Israel's future, we heard from David Wilder, who serves as Hebron's official spokesperson and is frequently cited in national media such as the BBC and *Jerusalem Post*. Wilder passionately described the situation of Jews who are fleeing other nations and pouring into Israel.

He told us, "We are seeing in Europe today an extreme influx of extreme Islam. In Scandinavia and France, the Jews are pouring out. They are scared. And they are going to come here [to Israel]. That is going to create a whole new situation in Israel. It is going to create new facts on the ground, a new reality. And *b'ezrat hashem*—with the help of God—we'll see the influx of Jews, we will see the coming of Messiah, we will see the building of the temple."

In the Six-Day War in 1967, the world remembers when the Jewish people were able to reunite the city of Jerusalem and gain access to their own Temple Mount for the first time in nearly 2,000 years. Leading Israeli archaeologist Dr. Gabriel Barkay, who is currently sifting through the mounds of material taken from under the Temple Mount, spoke of the importance of the 1967 war as we stood overlooking the Temple Mount in Jerusalem on a cool and windy spring day. He said, "First of all, you have to remember that the Temple Mount is the soul, heart and spirit of the Jewish people. It is the gem of Jerusalem, one of the most important sites in the history of the world, and the focus of the Judeo-Christian belief."

Yet in spite of all of their success in the past 60 years, the Jewish people and the modern State of Israel still face threats to their existence today.

In our documentary, we asked David Wilder, the spokesman at Hebron, the pointed question, "Can you be partners with the Palestinians right now?"

His response? One word: "No."

We then asked, "Can you have a peace process?"

His answer? "No, of course not."

When we asked him why not, there was no ambiguity in his assessment. Wilder said, "They want to kill us. They want to kill us, and they don't want us here. They say it again and again and again. Nonstop."

Yet Israel's leaders continue to reach out to the Palestinians in attempts to establish peace.

## A Monument to Fulfilled Biblical Prophecy

It has been 60 years of war and peace for those who live in Jerusalem. Yet their hopes for peace in Israel are changing. There is no better place to talk about the modern changes taking place in Israel than Ben Yehuda Street, in the heart of Jerusalem. As you walk along its modern shops and beautiful plazas, you can see evidence of the Jewish people who have come to Israel from 108 nations of the world. Every Israeli Independence Day, Ben Yehuda is one of the main places the Jewish people gather to celebrate the founding of the modern State of Israel.

As we strolled down this modern avenue, Jimmy shared, "John, here on Ben Yehuda Street, right in the middle of the New City of Jerusalem, it's a melting pot. Out of 108 nations of the world, Jews have come here to live in Israel in these last days. And on Friday afternoon many of them are here making their last-minute purchases before *Shabbat* [the Sabbath] begins.

"I've been on this same street on Independence Day when they have the celebration. This one little pedestrian street could probably take care of about 200,000 people. I've seen that many people out here. The celebration goes wild. It speaks of the importance for the Jewish people of the independence that was established for the Jewish state after its war of independence. Of course, the pronouncement that Israel was going to be a nation among the nations of the world took place at Independence Hall. Look at that small, two-story, window-front building that is now a Burger King. That used to be the Atari Café, on the lower story of the café, you would have Haganah, the fighting force, for the young Jewish nation.

"Upstairs on the second floor you would have the group of Menachem Begin and Yitzhak Shamir. They were referred to as 'The Underground.' And though they would not work in concert together, they would communicate between each other. They did it right here where the Burger King is today. This street is a reminder not only of the independence of the nation, but the wars of the nation as well."

As we walked through the crowds, Jimmy shared, "I'm reminded of one of the worst terrorist attacks ever to hit the Jewish people in the city of Jerusalem. It happened here on Ben Yehuda Street, just up the street where we were a moment ago. Today we have the police units here, and the anti-terrorist guys those over there on the big motor-cycles—those men are part of the most elite unit in all of Israel. It's here on this kind of a crowded street that terrorists, Palestinian fundamentalist Islamic terrorists, would come in trying to continue their struggle to get rid of the Jewish State of Israel."

Those attacks have been reduced to almost zero as a result of the elite military units on the street, and you could see it in the relaxed demeanor of the families walking there.

After we left Jerusalem we traveled to Tel Aviv, where Independence Hall resides. This is where it all started 60 years ago when David

Ben-Gurion read the Declaration of Independence of Israel on May 14, 1948, and the modern Jewish State of Israel was born.

As we approached the building, Jimmy explained, "Downtown here in the heart of Tel Aviv, the second most populated city in Israel, you can see all the industry, the banking and financial center, and different monuments [we passed a beautiful fountain and sculpture close to the hall] to those who built Tel Aviv. This city, they say, is the city where you play. You pray in Jerusalem, you study in Haifa, you play here in Tel Aviv."

Upon entering Independence Hall, it was clear we were walking into a place of utmost importance. We stepped off of the modern-day streets of Tel Aviv and were instantly taken back to the surroundings of 60 years ago in Independence Hall. As we entered the doors, we noticed the prophetic passage inscribed in the wall from Isaiah 35:1, which says, "The desert shall rejoice and blossom as the rose" (NKJV). On the opposite wall was a black-and-white picture of David Ben-Gurion.

On another wall was a mural that represented the people who have been coming from all over the world, the four corners of the earth. On that mural, we found the verse Jeremiah 31:8: "I will...gather them from the ends of the earth" (NKJV). We also remembered the next words in that chapter: God says, "They shall come and sing in the height of Zion" (Jeremiah 31:12 NKJV).

As we walked through the back rooms of the hall, we noticed additional pictures of emigrants coming from across the world to the Promised Land. One picture showed people packed into tent cities and coming off of ships from Europe.

We then walked into the hall itself, the physical location where the pronouncement was made declaring Israel a nation once again. There was a historic picture of Ben-Gurion in black and white with his shaggy hair flowing. The room was filled with wooden chairs surrounding a long table in the front. Each chair was marked with a number representing a specific Jewish leader. The ceiling stood two stories high, with no windows except for small panels at the top near the ceiling.

In the front of the room, the long rectangular table was covered by a blue tablecloth and set with three old-styled microphones. In the center rested a gavel.

We first listened to the retelling of the event in Hebrew while watching some of the Jewish guests listening intently. At the conclusion, the Israeli national anthem was played and everyone in the room stood up. The guests sang along proudly, some noticeably emotional and teary-eyed. At the conclusion, the room was quiet, and no one moved. Several moments of distinct silence left a profound impact on us as we prepared to conduct our interview.

After the guests emptied out, we stayed in the room where the modern nation of Israel began. With great passion, Israeli historical expert Itzik Dror told us, "This building was a historic building because Israel was born here. It was one of the greatest moments in the history of our people as our leaders announced to the world the new state, the modern-day State of Israel.

"This is where Israel was born sixty years ago. Let me show you the stage where it all happened. You see, this is where Ben-Gurion and his government were sitting. This is his chair. And you can see the microphones and even the gavel that he used to declare independence. At precisely 4:00 p.m. [on May 14, 1948] Israel was born."

Dror continued, "Now, it was a Friday and it was very important to start on time because the Shabbat was coming in, and you do not want to desecrate a Shabbat. This is why everything must start and be finished before the Shabbat. Also, the Egyptians were about to blitz the city. So at 4:00 p.m. exactly the ceremony began. Ben-Gurion picked up this small brown gavel and rapped three times on the table—three raps." Dror reenacted the act, sending a surprisingly loud echo throughout the hall. He then shared, "This would change, in my opinion, the history of the world and the fate of millions of people. What happened here, to my understanding, is as if the Jews opened the Bible and added another chapter to it. This is how I see it anyhow, and how Jewish people who sat here saw it."

In the hall were a set of historic pictures taken at the announcement and signing of the nation's founding document. When we asked Dror about these pictures, we quickly realized their importance was far greater than we first imagined.

Dror carefully picked them up and started to describe what we were looking at: "These are the pictures of the leaders of Israel when they signed the Document of Independence. You can see Golda Meir shaking hands with Moshe Sharett. This is Ben-Gurion here, and more pictures of the leaders of Israel shaking hands right after the declaration. Then, here is Ben-Gurion signing [the document]."

We stared in amazement as Dror showed one picture after another, all revealing a different part of the story. "People were so moved when Ben-Gurion signed the document of independence. They said it was the most important moment in their lives. You see Ben-Gurion here," Dror pointed out in the picture, "and the ministers of the temporary Jewish council. This was minutes before the actual declaration. Here are the ministers of the tiny cabinet, and more of Ben-Gurion actually reading the declaration."

Independence Hall. Itzik Dror (left) speaks to Jimmy DeYoung (center) and John Ankerberg (right). Photo © Alan Weathers.

Directing our attention to another picture, Dror's voice lifted. "Here we can see the street outside of the building. [What happened here] was supposed to be a secret. But it was not a secret. When Ben-Gurion came to the hall, half of Tel Aviv was standing outside." In the picture, you could see thousands of people packed in the street outside of the building. "You can see that it was something that brought everybody here to the streets." His tone then changed again. "It was very dangerous, because the Egyptians were about to blitz the city from the air.

"The Egyptians blitzed the city a few hours [later]. One of the reasons our leaders declared their independence in the heart of Tel Aviv in this room was because they were looking for safety. This room was considered a safe place."

We soon realized this "safe place" was really important, as Israel would soon be attacked from multiple directions.

## The Modern Nation Under Attack from Day One

When we spoke with Dror regarding the first attacks after Israel declared its independence, the interaction in our interview jumped a notch.

We asked, "And you were attacked on six different fronts?"

"Well, seven Arab armies participated in different numbers," answered Dror.

"Just a few hours after you did this?"

Dror revealed, "It was just a few *hours* after Ben-Gurion actually signed the Document of Independence." With this revelation, he returned to the pictures. "Here is Golda Meir again, signing the document. She had two kids, and her son came all the way from New York where he was studying music...She was a member of the temporary Jewish consulate. She was very high in the Jewish agency."

"And Golda Meir was sent to America by Ben-Gurion?"

"She was sent by Ben-Gurion. He was about to leave himself, but she told him, 'You cannot leave. I will go.' She came to America [in

1949] and raised an incredible amount of money for the new state—
$50 million in like a few weeks. It was simply amazing."

I (John) had remembered reading about this story when visiting
Israel for the first time 44 years ago. The account about Golda Meir's
crucial visit is shared in greater detail in the book *O Jerusalem!* After
Golda Meir's decision to leave for America, the book says that two
days later, Meir left for New York and then went to Chicago, where
she obtained permission to speak before a large gathering of influen-
tial Jewish leaders. She arrived in America with no luggage and only
the clothes she was wearing. The account tells of how she was the fifth
or sixth speaker of the evening:

> At the sight of her simple, austere figure moving to the
> speaker's stand, someone in the crowd murmured, "She
> looks like the women of the Bible." Then, without a text,
> the messenger [the plain-looking woman Ben-Gurion had
> sent] from Jerusalem began to speak.
>
> In a few months, she told her audience, "a Jewish state
> will exist in Palestine. We shall fight for its birth. That is
> natural. We shall pay for it with our blood. That is normal.
> The best among us will fall, that is certain. But what is
> equally certain is that our morale will not waver no matter
> how numerous our invaders may be."
>
> Yet, she warned, those invaders would come with cannon
> and armor. Against those weapons "sooner or later our cour-
> age will have no meaning, for we will have ceased to exist,"
> she said.
>
> "My friends," she said in making her plea, "we live in
> a very brief present. When I tell you we need this money
> immediately, it does not mean next month, or in two months.
> It means right now…"
>
> The woman who had arrived in the United States one
> bitter January night with ten dollars in her pocketbook
> would leave with fifty million…Waiting for her airplane

at Lydda Airport was David Ben-Gurion, the man who had wanted to go in her place…"The day when history is written," he solemnly told her, "it will be recorded that it was thanks to a Jewish woman that the Jewish state was born."[2]

But Golda Meir was not the only important figure in the photo. Dror proceeded to share information about the other individuals involved in this historic event. "These are the guests, the VIPs, like the rabbis, the chief rabbis of Israel, and other famous names. This man was the right hand of Theodor Herzl, a great Jewish leader who could not be here because he died a few years before. Here are pictures of Ben-Gurion holding the declaration—just three simple, ordinary sheets in his hand. There was not even enough time to write it nicely on a long scroll, as you would expect from a document of independence."

Interestingly, the document ended with these words: "Placing our trust in the 'Rock of Israel,' we affix our signatures to this proclamation." In the Old Testament, the Rock of Israel is none other than God Almighty.

## A Chosen Location

We interrupted at this point to ask, "Why was this building, Independence Hall, chosen?" We knew some of the reasons, but we wanted to hear what Dror would say.

"This building had a wonderful history. It was the first house of Tel Aviv and the art museum of the city. The reason they chose it was because of the windows. See the windows? This place is like a bomb shelter. Thick walls, concrete walls, and the high windows—they are two stories above us.

"Our leaders feared an aerial attack. This is why they chose to do it here." Pointing to another photograph, Dror explained, "This is one of the most famous pictures, where you can actually see the entire temporary Jewish council sitting here. Some of the chairs are empty because some of the members of the temporary council could not make it. In their journey to get here, they were caught behind enemy lines in the siege of Jerusalem.

"And this is the document of independence. There is a very good copy of it right here in the hall you can see. But this is a beautiful picture of the actual document with the red wax seal with the Star of David on it and thirty-seven signatures of the members of the temporary Jewish government. You can recognize Ben-Gurion's signature here along with Golda Meir's. They signed the document according to the first name of their family name." As we looked at the different signatures, he said, "This is how thirty-seven people signed the document."

## What Have We Experienced?

After our new friend had left, we took time to reflect on what we had experienced that warm spring day in Tel Aviv. I (John) shared, "It's very moving to actually be in the very room where history was made. You look at these chairs with the names of people on them, and all the folks who were at this desk, and realize they were literally risking their lives to be in this room. Yet when I see this room, I see more. Yes, we are here for the sixtieth anniversary of the modern State of Israel, but this is where it all started. To me, this building, this room, is a historical example, if you will, of prophecy being fulfilled in our generation. I can remember reading scholars who wrote about the fact that Israel would once again have to become a nation in the future according to the Scriptures, but they couldn't envision *how* it would happen. And when you hear these miraculous stories of how this little country came into being and was attacked from several different Arab states at the same time, it's incredible. It tells me that God was at work right in this room."

In so many different locations—17 Old Testament books on prophecy and the book of Revelation in the New Testament—the Bible explains how God would find the Jewish people wherever He had scattered them to the four corners of the earth. Remember the quote from Jeremiah 31 where He said that He will bring the people back? This event in this building is a monument to Bible prophecy.

I (Jimmy) noted, "Ezekiel talks about how God will gather the people in and of bones coming together saying, 'I will put flesh on the bones.' That's the restoration of the Jewish state after 2,000 years. And then God said, 'I will bring them to me.' God will bring the Jewish people to Him. But this [Israel's modern re-establishment] was a step in the process of all of that coming together. I don't know about you, but I'm a pretty emotional guy standing in a place like this.

"What happened here is an important part of the process toward that period of time when Jesus Christ comes back. The Declaration of Independence, their founding document for the modern state of Israel, was one of those benchmarks along the way. What a thrill to be here."

## The Reconstitution of Israel in Biblical Prophecy

Later, on the Mount of Olives (overlooking the Temple Mount), we talked about where the founding of the State of Israel fits into biblical prophecy.

Here, I (John) interviewed Jimmy, who is not only a journalist, but also a PhD in prophecy studies. I asked him, "Why was the founding of the State of Israel in 1948 of such huge importance on the biblical timeline of prophecy?"

Jimmy answered, "John, actually that is simply one chapter of the entire history of the Jewish people and a nation. You would have to go back four thousand years ago, when God picked a Gentile—Abraham of the Chaldees. He came over the Fertile Crescent here that was then known as Canaan, took him to a place called Hebron, and there God gave a promise to him that he would father a nation—that he would have a land."

In Genesis 17, we read that God appeared to Abraham and said, "I am God Almighty...I will establish my covenant as an everlasting covenant between me and you and your descendants after you for the generations to come, to be your God and the God of your descendants after you. The whole land of Canaan, where you are now an alien, I will give as an everlasting possession to you and your descendants after you; and I will be their God" (verses 1,7-8).

Jimmy continued, "That was the Abrahamic covenant. That was the beginning with Abraham establishing the first Jewish community four thousand years ago there in Hebron. And then as you trace Jewish history after Abraham with Isaac and Jacob, and then their descendants going into Egyptian bondage for some four hundred years, followed by the bringing of the children of Israel back into the land under the leadership of Joshua, you come to another dispersion when you come to the time of the Babylonian Empire, when Nebuchadnezzar destroys the temple, devastates the city, and takes the Jews into exile. But again the Jews come back into the land about seventy years later, as Jeremiah prophesied they would.

"Later, you come to the time of Jesus Christ, when the Roman Empire was in control of all of this property. Jesus Christ came, He lived, He died, He was buried, He rose again, and He went back to heaven. The Jews, about forty years after Jesus departed here, were dispersed, as Moses in Deuteronomy 28 said they would be. They were dispersed to the four corners of the earth. It had never happened that way before, as they went to Egypt in the first exodus, then came plagues, and God brought them back into the land. Then they went to the Babylonian captivity and they came back into the land under the leadership of the Persian King Cyrus.

"But the third time they were dispersed across the world and they would stay there for a two-thousand-year period of time. Yet Ezekiel 37 talks about a future time when the Jews would be gathered from out of the nations of the earth. And on a relief image on the menorah just in front of the Knesset is a picture of Ezekiel and the valley of dry bones. The relief features the prophecy in Ezekiel 37—the bones coming together, the flesh coming on the bones, and these flesh-covered bones standing up like a mighty army with the breath of life breathed into them.

"The truth is, back in chapter 34 of the book of Ezekiel the Lord says He will find His people wherever they have been scattered. He will search them out, and He will then gather them and bring them into the land. He will establish them in this land, the land of their forefathers, and He will feed them like a good shepherd feeds his flock. God says, 'I will' eighteen times in this text.

"And then Ezekiel 36 talks about the land. In fact, God tells the prophet Ezekiel, 'Preach to the land.' So thirty-five times in this chapter of the book of Ezekiel, we hear what the sovereign Lord says to the land: 'But you O mountains of Israel, will produce branches and fruit for my people, for they will soon come home. I will increase the number of men and animals on the land, and they will prosper on the land, and make it blossom like a rose.' In a very interesting verse in 36:22, the Lord says, 'It is not for your sake, O house of Israel, that I am going to do these things.' But then He says it is 'for the sake of my holy name.' When He could swear by nothing greater, He swore by His name. Concerning the last days, God says, 'I will take you out of the nations; I will gather you from all the countries and bring you back into your own land' (Ezekiel 36:24).

"That leads up to [Ezekiel] chapter 37 and verse 7, where it says the bones will come together. If you are not sure of what the bones are, [understand] this is apocalyptic literature. The Lord is using symbols to communicate an absolute truth. So what is the meaning of the symbolic bones that are being raised up? Verse 11 says, 'Then he said to me: "Son of man, these bones are the whole house of Israel."' He is talking about the Jewish people who have been scattered across the world, and like bones in a dry valley, they will be gathered together... Then God said, 'I will...make flesh come upon you and cover you with skin; I will put breath in you, and you will come to life. Then you will know that I am the LORD' (Ezekiel 37:6). Well, *that* is the restoration of a Jewish state."

A few moments before we had been standing at Independence Hall, where on May 14, 1948, the first prime minister of Israel, David Ben-Gurion, stood and announced to the world that the Jewish people had been restored as a nation. With the Bible open before us, we couldn't ignore what we saw all around us. For the first time in the modern history of the world, the people who had been scattered for 2,000 years had been regathered, and they had become a nation.

In our next chapter, we will continue our fascinating journey through Israel to discuss more of what the Bible says about *Israel Under Fire*. Together, we'll examine four clear promises God made to the Jewish people that every Christian should know and every skeptic should consider as evidence for the existence of God. The proof that these prophecies have come true comes directly from the land of Israel.

# Chapter 2

# A NATION REBORN

I n our last chapter, we reported that the sixtieth anniversary of the modern State of Israel is a monument to the fulfillment of biblical prophecy. We were in the heart of Tel Aviv at Independence Hall, where the official pronouncement resounded around the world from the lips of Israeli Prime Minister Ben-Gurion. But does the establishment of the modern State of Israel in our time have significance not just for the Jewish people, but for all people, including *us,* today?

The huge murals on the wall declare to everyone who enters that the Jewish prophets of old have conveyed in the past four promises to the Jewish people that every Christian should know about and every skeptic should consider as evidence for the existence of God:

- First, God promised through the prophets that in the last days He would gather the Jewish people from all over the world, from the different nations where they had been scattered.

- Second, God promised the Jewish people that He would gather them to a specific place: the land of Israel.

- Third, God promised the Jewish people that not only would He gather them to Israel, but He would make them into a nation once they arrived in the land.

- Fourth, God promised the Jewish people He would give them back their sacred city of Jerusalem.

In just one verse written by the prophet Ezekiel, you can find three of these four promises we mentioned earlier. God told the prophet Ezekiel in 570 B.C. what He will do in the future (Ezekiel 37:21-22 NASB):

1. He "will take the sons of Israel from among the nations where they have gone."
2. He "will gather them from every side and bring them into their own land."
3. He "will make them one nation in the land."

Twenty-five hundred years later, there can be no doubt that these three prophecies have come true in our generation.

God reiterated these same promises to other prophets. To Jeremiah, He said, "I will...gather them from the ends of the earth" (Jeremiah 31:8). Further, Jeremiah also predicted that in the future, God would make good on a fourth promise—namely, that the Jews would be given back their beloved city of Jerusalem. God said, "You are saying about this city, 'By the sword, famine and plague it will be handed over to the king of Babylon'; but this is what the LORD the God of Israel, says: 'I will...bring them back to this place [Jerusalem] and let them live in safety'" (Jeremiah 32:36-37).

## Independence Hall

It is one thing to read what God promised the Jewish people 2,500 years ago. It is another thing to realize we are living in the time period when God has fulfilled these four prophecies for the world to see. When we stood in Independence Hall, we were told many stories that confirmed that the events that brought the Jewish people together to establish Israel as a modern nation in 1948 were nothing short of miraculous.

We were fascinated when Dror told us about cadets from West Point who had attended one of his lectures: "They asked, 'We do not understand how you did this. Your top generals were just kids. What was the age of your troops?' And I said, 'Whoever could hold a rifle, down to the age of thirteen or eighteen. You know, we did whatever we could.'

"Further, you cannot explain how one tiny village forty miles from here stopped the entire Egyptian army from advancing to Tel Aviv. You cannot explain it! Maybe you can travel to Israel, see the scars on the wall, meet the people who fought that war, and they can give you an answer. I do not have an answer for you."

We left Independence Hall thinking about what God clearly said to the Jewish people through the prophet Ezekiel: "Thus says the Lord God, 'Behold, I will take the sons of Israel from among the nations where they have gone, and I will gather them from every side and bring them into their own land and I will make them one nation in that land'" (Ezekiel 37:21-22 NASB). No one can doubt any longer that these prophecies have been fulfilled in our lifetime exactly as God said. Further, the absolute proof that God has restored the Jewish nation was clear not only when we visited Independence Hall but in the following days when we visited the Knesset to talk with Israeli government leaders.

## The Fourth Promise

I then said to Jimmy, "God made another great promise to the Jewish people. He also promised to give them back their city of Jerusalem. And after they became a nation, it took them until the 1967 war before they would gain control of Jerusalem. How did that come about?"

Jimmy said, "The name *Jerusalem* is used 764 times in the entire Bible. Two passages come to mind immediately:

"One is Jeremiah 31, where God said He would give them their land back as well as their holy city of Jerusalem. The other is Psalm

132:13-14, which says, 'The LORD has chosen Zion [Jerusalem], he has desired it for his dwelling...forever and ever.' It's interesting that David Ben-Gurion said, 'Jerusalem is the eternal undivided capital city for the Jewish people.' And on June 7, 1967—after almost two thousand years of a divided city—the Jewish people were able to reunite their city, where it is now their eternal undivided capital city."

Yet from our own personal experiences in Israel, we both knew the Jewish people are still under further attack, and the Bible makes some sober predictions about the days to come, including a future battle over the city of Jerusalem. In fact, the Bible teaches in Zechariah 12:2 that in the last days, the city of Jerusalem is going to become a "cup of trembling" (KJV). This phrase likely indicates that Jerusalem is going to make men act like they are intoxicated after drinking strong wine. The leaders of the nations will act out of control. This will cause a major battle for possession of the most important city to the Jewish people, and in particular, the Temple Mount itself, and the nations of the world are going to try to take even Jerusalem away from the Jewish people.

So biblically, and in our news today, Jerusalem is the center focus of the world's attention. It is the city that God gave to the Jewish people, and the location where God said He is going to dwell among the Jewish people forever. In the coming chapters, we will examine the future battles God predicts will come to this city in the future.

To begin, we will travel to the four borders of Israel to assess the past political and military history of the nations bordering Israel and the threat these nations pose to Israel today. Then we will sit down with Israel's leaders and hear how they view the current and future threats from their neighbors, and the dreams they have for their own people.

# Chapter 3

# A LAND RESETTLED

I (John) wanted to visit the famous city of Hebron, inside Israel's borders, to see the place where God brought Abraham 4,000 years ago and gave him the Abrahamic covenant. Hebron is a small town situated some 22 miles southwest of Jerusalem, and it is the site of many recent violent incidents. The Bible tells us that when Abraham's wife Sarah died, he buried her in the cave of Machpelah in Hebron, which Abraham bought from Ephron the Hittite (Genesis 23). Hebron is another historic landmark in Jewish history, because Abraham, Isaac, Jacob, and their families were all buried here.

We were told that when we traveled to Hebron, we would have to ride in an armor-plated bus and enter at our own risk. In May 1980, Palestinian terrorists murdered six Jewish yeshiva (seminary) students and wounded 20 others who were returning from prayers at the Tombs of the Patriarchs. In February 1994, Dr. Baruch Goldstein opened fire on Muslim worshipers at the tomb, murdering 29 and wounding 125. Goldstein was subsequently killed by survivors in the mosque.

Our television crew was very quiet as we packed all of our expensive cameras and lights into the bus. As we approached the city, we passed through a series of checkpoints covered in barbed wire and protected by numerous armed guards. As we slowly wound through the streets entering the city, we noticed that many of the buildings had walls missing and were marked with bullet holes. We were met by Mr. David Wilder, the official spokesman for the Jewish community at Hebron, who accompanied us into the city.

Wilder climbed on the bus with us, and as we rode along, Jimmy, who knew David, began by asking, "David, aren't we now just making our way up to the archaeological remains of the original city of Hebron? How far back do the ruins date?"

David quickly responded, "Back to 4,300 to 4,500 years ago. It goes back a long time."

When Abraham left Ur of the Chaldeans, he made his way up over the Fertile Crescent and came down through what we know as the southern part of the State of Israel today, ending up right here in Hebron. As Wilder explained during our interview, "That's probably where we're driving now and where Abraham walked around. And this was all a big field then—it was all open. They didn't have houses or anything else. But this is it; this is the roots not only of the Jewish people, but of all monotheism."

Jimmy asked, "And wasn't this particular location not only where Abraham had the opportunity to establish a Jewish community, but the place where God gave him the Abrahamic covenant? Is this the same place?"

"Of course. This is where he received the promises from God." As we listened our eyes were glued to the gently sloping fields around us.

As we approached the city, it looked in many ways like we were entering a war zone. We were surprised to discover that about 500 Israelis live in Hebron, consisting of 90 families with over 350 children. On the outskirts of the city of Hebron, another 7,500 Jewish people live with their families. And surrounding the small number of Jewish people in the city are 166,000 Palestinians.

Israeli soldiers with machine guns guard the inhabitants of Hebron night and day. Groups of four or five soldiers were only a few feet away from us and our film crew for all of our interview. As we came into the main part of the city, we were struck by the sight of a gigantic mosque that had been built by Muslims over the place where Abraham, Isaac, Jacob, and their families are all buried.

Jimmy asked, "Are the Jews allowed to go into the mosque?"

Wilder answered, "Into part of it, but that site was off limits to Jews and to Christians for seven hundred years. The first building on top of the caves was built two thousand years ago by Herod when he was king of Judea. Back in 1260, Crusaders were expelled from Hebron by the Mamluks [slaves raised to be Islamic soldiers who served the Muslim caliphs], and a Mamluk leader closed off the Temple Mount [as well as Hebron]; and that aside lasted for seven hundred years. Only when we [the Jewish settlers] came back in 1967 did we again have access to this site. And it's very important to note that our neighbors [the Palestinians] tell us that if they should ever control Hebron again they won't let us [the Israelis] in. They won't let me in, and they won't let you [as Christians] in…If the Arabs should ever control it they won't let anybody who is not a Muslim go into the tomb area because they say that it's a mosque, and only Muslims can pray there."

## Why Do People Stay?

As we walked up the hill guarded by different groups of soldiers with machine guns every 40 feet, we wondered, "Why do these Jewish people choose to live with their families in these dangerous areas? What draws them here?"

Wilder responded, "This is where we all started. It's very difficult to get closer to the roots of the Jewish people and monotheistic belief than right here. You can't get any closer. People say, 'How can you live here? Why do you live here?' And I say, 'Look, if you take a tree and you cut off the roots, what happens to the tree? It dies.'

"In 1929 the Jews were expelled from Hebron. They came back in 1931, and they were here until 1936. Then they were thrown out again. In 1948 we lost Jerusalem. Later, when we came back to Jerusalem, the very next day we came back to Hebron. Jerusalem and Hebron— they go together; you lose your roots, everything else dries up."

We learned that Hebron is the second most sacred location in Israel for the Jewish people. As mentioned, it was here that the Abrahamic covenant was given to Abraham. He later purchased a cave to be used as a burial site for his wife and himself. Later, Isaac and his wife and Jacob and his wife were buried at the same site.

Today, Hebron is the "last stand" as far as the Jewish people are concerned. With only 5,000 Israelis in the community of Hebron surrounded by about 166,000 Palestinians—many of them members of Hamas, the Islamic fundamentalist terrorist element, every moment is tense.

During our interview, Wilder mentioned a funeral he had to attend for the killing of a small child in that Jewish community. The child was killed by a sniper bullet just a few feet from where we were taping the interview. I (John) thought, *Then why are we standing in the open on this hill doing this interview?* We discovered the Jewish people endure all types of harassment by the Palestinians, who are trying to drive them out of the area. The Jewish people at Hebron feel that if they are going to exist as a Jewish state, they must take a stand in Hebron and other biblical sites where God spoke to the patriarchs and promised to give them the land and these sacred places forever.

## Hebron as a Monument to Biblical Prophecy

We believe Hebron is a monument today to the fulfillment of biblical prophecy because it is the place where God promised to give Abraham and his physical descendants the land of Israel. I (John) took out my Bible while there and opened it to Genesis 15:7-18, where God said to Abraham, "I am the LORD, who brought you out of Ur of the Chaldeans to give you this land to take possession of it...To your descendants I give this land, from the river of Egypt to the great river, the Euphrates."

When Abraham was 99 years old God promised him, "I will establish my covenant as an everlasting covenant between me and you and your descendants after you for the generations to come, to be your God and the God of your descendants after you. The whole land of Canaan, where you are now an alien, I will give as an everlasting possession to you and your descendants after you; and I will be their God" (Genesis 17:7-8).

It is apparent these promises from God were not temporary or conditional, but everlasting and irrevocable. God confirmed the same covenant promises later to Isaac and Jacob.

We then asked David Wilder, "Do you have to defend the right of Jewish people to live in these communities—in what is biblically called Judea and Samaria?"

"Yes, we have a difficult task. The task we have is to defend the Jewish rights over the heartland of the land of Israel, over the biblical parts in which our ancestors—our fathers Abraham, Isaac, Jacob, King David—lived and built the first Jewish national homeland. We have returned to places like the city of Hebron, the city of Shechem, also known as Nablus, and Shiloh, where the Ark was located. When you live in Judea and Samaria, you live in the midst of history—the most sacred, the most important period of our history. And unfortunately, we also have to deal with the present realities, and we have to defend our right to be here."

## The Palestinian Position

Many people do not realize that today over 200 Jewish settlements (many of which are founded on well-known biblical historical sites) are at the center of controversy in the Middle East peace process. The Palestinian position is that all of the Israeli settlements should be dismantled. If some are to remain, they must fall under the sovereignty of the Palestinian Authority. The Israeli position, however, is that no existing settlements should be uprooted.

For the Palestinian perspective on the Jewish settlements, we sat down and interviewed Mr. Adnan Husseini, the official spokesman for the Palestinian Liberation Organization in Jerusalem and the presidential adviser (to Mahmoud Abbas) on Jerusalem affairs. He is also one of Yasser Arafat's cousins. Speaking on behalf of the Palestinians, Mr. Husseini steadfastly maintains that the Jewish settlements are nothing more than "an obstacle to peace."

Mr. Husseini specifically stated in our interview together, "Everywhere you go [in the Jewish settlements], you see the street is closed. Look now at the cities. Go to Hebron—the 166,000 people in Hebron. Go to the entrance, and [you will] see it was a huge entrance and they [the Israelis] made it like a barricade...And they build everything, you know, to dissolve the [Palestinian] cities and the people...[the actions of the Israelis] will never bring peace and will never allow the settlers of Israel to be secure. This is exactly the opposite way to do things... This is clear. And President Abbas says it. If there is a small [Jewish] settlement or big settlement, it's illegal."

I (Jimmy) politely asked Mr. Husseini, "At what time in history was it that you believe the Jewish people came in and took away your rights to the nation that was here? How did that unfold?"

He answered, "We used to live in Jerusalem in 1948. And when Mr. Ben-Gurion annexed west Jerusalem, illegally, violating the international laws, you know, and the laws which established his state, people [Palestinians] fled from there. And they [the Israelis] put their hands on these properties.

"And after 1948 when it was established, the State of Israel, with the promises that this is the beginning of this state, and the state is now here, you know, they fabricated the story here and there really. But this State of Israel is not the fact; it's really a lie."

As we listened to Mr. Husseini speak, we couldn't help but think he was revising history. After our interview with him, Jimmy and I discussed the historical questions.

Jimmy noted that Mr. Husseini would have a lot of difficulty documenting that there was ever a Palestinian state in that location. Regarding the state that was allegedly taken from them, who were the leaders of that state? Where was its capital city? Give us the details. Mr. Husseini had also talked about 1917 being the time when the Jews started to steal this piece of land known as Palestine. But in 1917, it was England that took control of the land. General Allenby had defeated the Turks, who had controlled that land since the 1500s, and therefore in 1917 the British were in charge of the land, not the Jewish people. This remained unchanged until November 27, 1949, when the United Nations granted the Jewish people the right to have a homeland.

According to the U.N. plan, the piece of land was to be divided. The plan was to give one portion to the Palestinians and another to the Jews. But the Palestinians rejected that plan. In fact, the Palestinian leaders told their women, children, and elderly, "Leave the country. Just go over across the Jordan River into Jordan. We will wipe out this new nation. The Jews are only six hundred thousand people. You will be back in a couple of weeks, and we will continue to live here in Palestine."

But the Palestinians did *not* push those Jews into the Mediterranean as they predicted they would, and the Jewish people were victorious in that War of Independence. Others say the Jewish people never actually won. The War of Independence is continuing on because the Palestinian people continue to fight the Jews even though the Jews have made attempts to coexist and give the Palestinians a state. Yet up to this day the Palestinians still reject the two-state proposal and what the Jewish people are offering. They don't want to coexist. They want all the land.

I (John) remembered a reference Mr. Husseini made regarding the 1967 war: "It is very clear that if King Hussein of Jordan had not interfered in the war of 1967, the Palestinians today would not be confined to occupying the West Bank."

I asked Jimmy about this and he responded, "If he is referring to the 1967 war, that war was real. In fact, from the north, the Syrians attacked the Jewish nation of Israel. From the south, Egypt attacked. King Hussein of Jordan did not want to come into the war. He was duped by the leader of Egypt into joining the war. He was told by the Egyptians, 'We are dying; if you don't enter the war right now, we're going to be totally destroyed.' That brought King Hussein in and he attacked Israel. And all Israel did was protect itself. Israel drove the Egyptians back to the Sinai Desert and set up a buffer zone. Israel drove the Jordanians back across the east side of the Jordan River and set up a buffer zone. Israel also drove out the Syrians from the Golan Heights to set up a buffer zone. The Israelis were trying to protect themselves; that is no myth. And in six days they defeated their enemies. That's a miracle of God."

Christians certainly understand why many of the Jewish people feel God gave them the divine right to live on such lands as Hebron and other biblical sites, and to live in the land of Israel itself. Yet in spite of the historical and biblical background, and in spite of the legal right of the Jewish settlers to live in Hebron, it may come as a surprise to Christians that Hebron and other settlement sites have constantly been placed on the negotiating table in the Middle East peace process.

I (Jimmy) asked David Wilder, "What would happen if indeed the Palestinians were victorious and were able to get this piece of land as part of their state? Would you and others in the Jewish community stay and continue to live here?"

Wilder said, "I don't see anybody picking up and leaving. This is our home. I don't think it's going to happen. God didn't bring us back to the land of Israel after two thousand years of exile to throw us out again. And He didn't bring us back to our roots, to a place like Tel Hebron, which is property that we've owned, legally, since the beginning of the 1800s. But we've owned it in reality since four thousand years ago. He didn't bring us back here to say, 'OK guys, take off.' So I don't think that's going to happen."

## The Issue Is Personal

For Wilder, the issue is deeply personal. When asked whether the Palestinians have a desire to enter a peace agreement with Israel, he answered not only from a strategic standpoint, but a personal one as well. In his words, the Palestinians mean what they say when they declare violence. "Two months ago, in my apartment—my house down in Beit Hadassah—somebody started shooting, and there is a hole in my son's clothing cabinet—*in the door of the cabinet.* Fortunately for us it was 10:30 in the morning and no one was home. If my son had been standing there...God forbid! Last week a rock, a huge rock, went through the window of one of my neighbor's homes. People continue to be attacked."

As American Christians taping in Israel and interviewing a Jewish man who had come to live in Israel, it was fascinating to hear Wilder say, "I know that God has a plan, and I know that we are part of His plan. I know that we came back here for a reason. He is implementing that plan, and we are part of it. And we are going to reach that and we are going to see all of the Jewish people come to the land of Israel. Somebody asked me a few days ago, 'Well, what is your solution [to the Jewish settlement problem]?' And I said 'When you come and live here, and you know if instead of having ten thousand people in Gush Katif [the Gaza Strip area], there had been fifty thousand people, they never could have thought of throwing them out. The same is true here in Hebron.'

"And [Jews returning to Israel will help], and they are going to come. We are seeing in Europe today an extreme influx of extreme Islam. In Scandinavia and France the Jews are pouring out. They are scared. And they are going to come here. And that is going to create a whole new situation in Israel. It is going to create new facts on the ground, a new reality. And *b'ezrat hashem*—with the help of God—we'll see the influx of Jews, we will see the coming of Messiah, we will see the building of the temple."

Wilder shared his views as a spokesperson only for the Jewish community in Hebron, yet his views are held by many others in the 200 Jewish settlements all over Israel today. There is abundant evidence that devout Jews in Israel continue to seek for the return of the Jewish people to Israel and ultimately the coming of Messiah and the rebuilding of their temple. However, their hopes and desires to rebuild the temple conflict with the location of the gold-domed shrine on the Temple—the Dome of the Rock—which 1.5 billion Muslims hold sacred.

In the next chapter, we'll explore the Temple Mount itself and discover how volatile the situation is for the Jewish people—and for every person on the planet—today.

Chapter 4

# A CITY REUNITED

I n this chapter, we will take you to two amazing sites—the original City of David, and the world-famous yet controversial Temple Mount. Anyone who visits Jerusalem can see both sites today.

Secularists are surprised to learn that the Bible is still the historical guidebook for anyone who visits the land of Israel. Archaeology has shown that the Jewish people described in the Bible lived in this very city of Jerusalem. The geographical places mentioned in the Bible can be seen and visited here. Artifacts bearing inscriptions of each of the time periods and many of the names of the people in the Bible have been found here. Some of the oldest and most important writings in the world have been discovered near here. The Dead Sea Scrolls have proven how accurately the Bible was written and preserved, and have provided further evidence of the events that happened here. We visited the original site of the City of David to learn how prophecy has been fulfilled in the past and to visit the Temple Mount, one of the places the Bible predicts will be in the news worldwide in the future.

## On the Road to Jerusalem

Our first stop was the winding Kidron Valley, which runs along the Eastern wall off the Old City of Jerusalem and separates the Temple

Mount from the Mount of Olives. The Kidron Valley runs east down through the Judean Desert, all the way to the Dead Sea. As we stood in the excavations of the original City of David, just south of the Temple Mount, we looked across the Kidron Valley, to the Mount of Olives and to Silwan, a modern Palestinian village. We stood on a high knoll, not far from the southern steps of the temple, and looked down on ten acres representing the original city of Jerusalem, dating back some 3,000 years.

King David had been the king of the tribe of Judah and had, at first, located in Hebron for about seven-and-a-half years. But then all of the other 11 tribes came to ask him to become king of the entire nation. As a result, David came to the Jebusite stronghold, known today as Jerusalem, and had an opportunity to capture the stronghold and did so. He then established Jerusalem as the political capital for the Jewish people.

That was 3,000 years ago. Longevity of time gives the Jewish people evidence as to the reason why they can claim this city is their city. From Kiriath-Jearim, which is out west toward Tel Aviv, David brought the Ark of the Covenant into Jerusalem. He placed the Ark of the Covenant right in the City of David near a place where we were standing, which is visible to all those who visit the site. The Ark was kept there until King Solomon, David's son, built the first Jewish temple on top of Mount Moriah. However, today, on Mount Moriah, one can see a pewter-colored mosque known as the al-Aqsa Mosque. About 100 yards to the north of the mosque stands a huge gold-domed building, the Dome of the Rock, an Islamic shrine. It sits on the peak of Mount Moriah where King Solomon built the first Jewish temple.

Many people do not know this, but David's house sat lower on the Temple Mount than the Jewish temple. This showed his humility to God and the temple.

## The Davidic Covenant

It was in David's house in Jerusalem that God responded to David's request to build *God* a house, a temple to dwell in. The Bible records the following:

> The word of the LORD came to Nathan, saying: "Go and tell my servant David, 'This is what the LORD says: Are you the one to build me a house to dwell in? …The LORD declares to you that the LORD himself will establish a house for you. When your days are over and you rest with your fathers, I will raise up your offspring to succeed you, who will come from your own body, and I will establish his kingdom. *He is the one who* will build a house for my Name, and I will establish the throne of *his kingdom forever*…Your house and your kingdom will endure *forever* before me; your throne will be established *forever*." Then King David went in and…said, "Who am I, O Sovereign LORD, and what is my family, that you have brought me this far? And as if this were not enough in your sight, O Sovereign LORD, *you have also spoken about the future of the house of your servant*…" (2 Samuel 7:4-5,11-13,16,18-19, italics added).

Notice how many times God promised David that the kingdom of one of his future descendants would last forever. This promise of God to David is called the Davidic covenant—it's one of the key passages in Scripture regarding the coming of the Messiah, one of David's future descendants. This promise is also a clarification and an expansion of God's promises to Abraham.

The word "house" here not only meant a human house, meaning David's family, but also pointed to David's future son, the Messiah: "He is the one who will build a house for my name, and I will establish the throne of his kingdom forever."

Second, it meant a temple: "Are you the one to build me a house?"

And third, it meant a dynasty. For example, the current British royal family is called "the house of Windsor." God said to David, "Your house and your kingdom will endure forever before me." Some of God's promise was fulfilled in Solomon, but part awaits the future and can apply only to Jesus Christ. Why? Because God states that David's throne will endure forever, and that David's house and kingdom will be established forever. But David does not have a descendant upon his throne today. And there is no throne in Jerusalem. So, did God not fulfill His promises? No. God clearly states in Psalm 89:34-36:

> I will not break my covenant or go back on what I promised. Once and for all I have vowed by my own holiness, I will never deceive David. His dynasty will last forever. His throne will endure before me (NET).

God's promise to David will be fulfilled in the future, when Jesus Christ, one of the descendants of David, returns. As we stood on the upper porch of David's original house, I (Jimmy) noted, "King Solomon would have had a house next to David's. It is interesting to point out that it took King Solomon seven-and-a-half years to build the temple. It took him *thirteen-and-a-half years* to build his own house, and his house was very opulent. But that was the way King Solomon was."

## The Bible Behind the Geography

When David was king and walked across his patio, what would he have looked upon? We happened to be standing in the same location. Because I (Jimmy) have led numerous tours over the years throughout Israel, I explained, "Across the Kidron Valley, a little to the right of the Mount of Olives over there, is Silwan, an Arab village. If you were to go on beyond that village over to the other side of the Mount of Olives, you would arrive at Bethany, where Mary, Martha, and Lazarus lived. Jesus spent much time with them. In fact, every time He came to Jerusalem, He would stay with this dear family. As you come back over the Mount of Olives, you see in front of us a large Jewish cemetery. Now, Jewish people desire to be buried in that cemetery because they believe that one day, the Messiah, according to Zechariah 14:4, will step down on the Mount of Olives. Some of them have even given up to a million dollars for a burial plot there so they can meet the Messiah when He comes back. They believe they will then be resurrected and meet the Messiah face to face.

"Going up the slopes and to the top of the Mount of Olives, you can see a tower. And that tower is the Church of Ascension, the traditional site for where Jesus Christ is said to have ascended into the heavenlies."

I then pointed a little to the left of the Mount of Olives and said, "As we continue along, we see over here a gold, spiral-domed church that is a Russian Orthodox church. It was built by the last czar of Russia for his mother. Her patron saint was Mary Magdalene. What is special about that is the fact Mary Magdalene was the first one to come to the gravesite of Jesus Christ."

As we stood on the top of the City of David, we turned to our left and could see the Temple Mount nearby and the wall surrounding it. Pointing there, I explained, "First, high above the valley, is a very high wall jutting out that drops directly to the road below in the Rift Valley. The pinnacle of the temple is where Jesus was tempted. Satan brought Him here and told Him that if He cast Himself off the wall, He could have the kingdoms of the world.

"Next, you see the southern retaining wall of the Temple Mount. King Herod used about ten thousand slaves to build this southern retaining wall. At the pinnacle there you can go down the eastern retaining wall running parallel along the Kidron Valley. From this vantage point we can't see it, but the Eastern Gate stands directly across from the Mount of Olives. You can see from here where the Hulah Gates, the gates almost directly facing us as we look at the Temple Mount, would have been when the Jewish worshippers would have gone up onto the Temple Mount. In front of that area were all types of ritual baths, called the mikvah. And before going into the temple, the Jewish worshippers would go and take a ritual bath. They had to walk seven steps down into what they referred to as living water—water that was either running water or rain water. And they would take a ritual bath, then go up onto the Temple Mount to worship."

## The Temple Mount

Next, we gazed at the Temple Mount itself. I (Jimmy) attempted to portray how the Jewish temple originally looked. "Protruding above the skyline of modern Jerusalem is the Muslim-controlled Dome of the Rock, which is a Muslim shrine. Underneath this Muslim shrine is the exact location of the Holy of Holies, according to ninety-seven percent of orthodox Jewish scholarship.

"The temple itself would have stood on that piece of ground, and the cupola, just to the east of it, was the place of an altar two stories high. That is where all the animals would have been sacrificed. The height of the door that opened up into the temple itself was approximately five stories high. The temple itself would have been anywhere between seventeen and twenty-one stories high. The difference in height depends on the exact length of measurement of a cubit, which ranged from seventeen to twenty-one inches long.

"The Temple Mount is the most sacred piece of property in the world. Jews consider it a sacred location, as do Muslims. Christians believe it is where Jesus Christ will come back to earth to rule and reign. The Bible teaches Jesus will come back by way of the Mount of Olives across the Kidron Valley, enter the Eastern Gate, and walk into the Holy of Holies. Ezekiel 43:7 says, 'I will dwell among the sons of Israel forever. And the house of Israel will not again defile My holy name'" (NASB).

As we looked just south of the Dome of the Rock, we looked on the pewter-domed building called the al-Aqsa Mosque. When Muslims refer to the entire Temple Mount, they don't call it the Temple Mount. They call it al-Aqsa. And that building is the al-Aqsa Mosque, the only mosque on the Temple Mount. That is where Muslims come for their sermons and for their worship on their holy day, which is Friday.

I continued, "Just beyond the al-Aqsa Mosque is the huge gold-domed building called the Dome of the Rock, where the First and Second temples stood. When King David, who lived in Jerusalem, the City of David, wanted to build the temple here, God would not allow him to. David had purchased the land, which was then a threshing floor. He took that threshing floor and prepared it to be the Holy of Holies.

"The Bible tells us that the son of King David, King Solomon, who was the third king of Israel, was the one allowed to build the temple on the Temple Mount. Solomon brought the Ark of the Covenant from the City of David, which was right next to the Temple Mount, and took it into the newly built new temple. The temple was built on the very same spot that Abraham offered his son Isaac."

## The Future of Jerusalem

In the future, this piece of sacred real estate will continue to hold prophetic significance for God's people. The short version of the prophetic events that will take place at this location when Jesus Christ comes back to earth includes Jesus arriving on earth. He will come with those of us who know Christ as Lord and Savior, who were raptured from earth to heaven, spent seven years in the heavens with Him during the terrible Tribulation on earth, and will come back with Him to earth at this very spot in Jerusalem. The armies of the world will gather throughout the Kidron Valley, surrounding Jerusalem, for the Battle of Armageddon. Then when Jesus returns, His enemies will flee.

The Bible says the mountain range will open up a way for the Jewish people to make their way 97 miles north, through the middle part of the nation to the Jezreel Valley. In the Jezreel Valley, the armies of the world will prepare for war. During the time of the seven years of Tribulation, before the armies of the world gather at Jerusalem, two out of every three Jews will be killed according to Zechariah 13:8. Given the present population of Israel, that would leave about four million people. Jesus will go to Petra, where God has provided a place for the Jews. He will bring about four million Jews across the Kidron Valley and enter that Eastern Gate. He will come to the temple, walk into the Holy of Holies, and sit down to rule as King of kings and Lord of lords.

As we just mentioned, the Bible predicts there is a coming time when the world will gather against Israel. It is time for us now to examine that which will bring Israel under fire—the alignment of the nations.

During our travels, we visited the borders of the four nations surrounding Israel, and we took our television crew along to capture the way these borders look today. We also discussed the significant prophetic events that are related to each of Israel's neighbors. As you'll quickly see, many of the Bible prophecies related to future events are rapidly approaching fulfillment today.

In Israel, the Jewish people are constantly preparing to defend their country in case war breaks out. At the same time, there is a great yearning for peace. Peace is talked about all the time, with certain world leaders vowing to give their full attention to bringing peace. U.S. President Barack Obama has openly stated that he hopes to pursue peace in the Middle East. Ban Ki-moon, the current secretary general of the United Nations, has made the remarkable statement that "my number one priority is to bring a resolution to the Israeli–Palestinian conflict." So the hopes for peace will also be part of our conversation in the following chapters. Toward that end, you will hear directly from those leaders in Israel who are striving for peace while preparing for the worst. Further, we will try to accurately answer the questions, Is there going to be peace in the Middle East anytime soon? And what does the Bible have to say about that matter?

# PART TWO

# THE ALIGNMENT OF THE NATIONS AGAINST ISRAEL

# Chapter 5

## AN ALIGNMENT REFORMED

Over the years, I (John) have been impressed with the fact that Jimmy has interviewed every Israeli prime minister since 1993, in addition to numerous cabinet members and other Israeli political and religious leaders. In my travels to Israel over the years, I have had opportunity to interview top scholars in Israel. But during this trip, we specifically sought answers from political and military leaders on one question: What is the number one threat to the existence of Israel today?

Israeli Prime Minister Benjamin Netanyahu kindly offered us the opportunity to sit with a select group of journalists for an interview on this topic.[3] He began, "I think we have to do everything in our power to prevent the arming of Iran with nuclear weapons. On this, I have to say, there is absolute unanimity in Israel."

We also spoke with Moshe Arens, who served three terms as Israel's minister of defense, one of the most important and stress-filled jobs in the Middle East. He stated, "Nuclear capability in the hands of the Iranians is not only a threat against Israel, it is a threat to the whole world." All through our 21 interviews, we were consistently and firmly told that Iran is the major threat against Israel, according to the Israeli intelligence community and as far as the Jewish State of Israel is concerned. But Iran is not the only nation that threatens their existence.

As Netanyahu explained, "We're not only being told that we'll be wiped off the face of the earth [by Iran], but also that Iranian-backed proxies [Hezbollah in Lebanon, Hamas in Gaza] are establishing themselves at our doorsteps and rocketing our people." In a moment, you will hear just how many rockets are now aimed at Israel by its enemies on their borders.

U.S. military experts agree that Israel is facing multiple threats today. Retired U.S. Lieutenant General Jerry Boykin noted, "I think it's only a matter of time until there will be another attack out of south Lebanon, again supported by the Syrians, as well as the Iranians." Unfortunately, his predictions have already turned true as border battles between Hamas in Lebanon [including rocket attacks] and northern Israel have escalated repeatedly in recent months.

There are many people who want to know how to interpret today's news headlines in light of what the Bible predicts will happen in the future. What nations are specifically mentioned in Bible prophecy as having a role in the end-time scenario in Israel? And what do military and political leaders believe about the threats from radical Islam? Are they just threats to Israel, or to other nations as well? According to Boykin, who worked for a number of years in counterterrorism, "People say this is a war of ideas. No, this is just like every other war— it's a war for terrain. And that terrain is the whole world. And radical Islam is a threat to the entire world. It is now the fastest-growing religion worldwide."

Benjamin Netanyahu was even tougher in his assessment. We have him on tape saying, "Militant Islam rejects any territorial or political solution. It wants the dissolution of the State of Israel. And this is the problem; this is the source of the problem. This is why it's becoming so dangerous, because *how can you negotiate with somebody who wants your destruction?*" (italics added).

Yet this is just the tip of the iceberg of what the Bible says Israel will face in the future.

## Exploring Israel

As you look down at the nation of Israel from space, you come to realize just how small it is. Israel stretches only 263 miles from north to south, and its width ranges from 71 miles at its widest point to only 9 miles at its narrowest point. To the northeast, Israel faces a 47-mile border with Syria; to the north, a 49-mile border with Lebanon. To the east, Israel has a 147-mile border with Jordan, and to the southwest, Israel borders Egypt. Directly south, Israel has a small window onto the Red Sea.

If Israel looks small on a map, it feels even more so when you drive through it. We traveled by Land Rover with our television crew to all four borders of Israel, and were shocked to realize how "locked in" Israel is to the nations surrounding her. Did you know it's possible to drive to all four borders of Israel in a single 15-hour day?

We took a trip into the Judean wilderness, close to the Jordanian border and only a few miles from the Dead Sea. To begin, I (John) asked Jimmy to explain the view of the location in the wilderness about a 30-minute drive from Jerusalem. He said, "I want you to know the historical significance of this place, plus the political pressures Israel is experiencing from its neighbors. See, you have over there the Dead Sea—the northern end of the Dead Sea. It stretches south for about 67 miles, with the Jordan Valley extending past that all the way down to the Red Sea, which forms the southernmost border of Israel. The entire Jordanian border with the state of Israel is 147 miles long." Jimmy then pointed to the east and said, "You have Jordan over there—Amman, Jordan, which is only 25 miles away. Back over here to the west, you have Jerusalem, which is about 15 miles away."

"How far up to Jerusalem?" I asked.

"We are talking about 15 miles from here."

"How far is the Jordanian border?"

"Well, it is only about 15 miles, too."

"Fifteen miles. That's really close. So we are about an hour from the capital city in Jordan?"

"Yes. From Jerusalem to Amman, it's only about an hour's drive. And in a jet aircraft, minutes."

I remembered something I had researched earlier: "I heard that if Israel was under surprise attack, it would take less than five minutes for a jet to lift off from Jordan and cross into Israel, and only ten minutes for planes to lift off and fly from Syria into Israeli airspace. That is all the time Israel has to defend itself, and it takes Israel three minutes to get a plane off the ground." That's also why Israel's military always has some planes in the air.

Jimmy went on. "Israel is living in a tough neighborhood. And that's what I want everyone to comprehend as we visit the borders of Israel. The nations that would like to rid the world of the Jewish people are very close indeed."

I then asked Jimmy, "Explain how Israel is hemmed in by people who are not friendly to them."

"On the south you have Egypt. Over here to the east you have Jordan. They say they are somewhat friendly, but there is an Islamic movement in Jordan that's becoming very radical. To the northeast you have Syria, and directly north you have Lebanon. And to the west, of course, you have the Mediterranean. So Israel is locked in tight on this piece of real estate—it is the land bridge between three continents: Africa, Asia and Europe. The people of Israel are locked in, with enemies surrounding them."

The close proximity of the different nations to Israel is stunning to Americans. They are used to vast amounts of land separating them from anyone else and from any danger. But Americans are now starting to get an idea of the danger of close proximity with drug trafficking along our border with Mexico. But unlike Israel, we don't have rockets fired at us on a daily basis, either. This problem for Israel was confirmed by Israeli Prime Minister Benjamin Netanyahu when he talked to us very plainly about Israel's neighbors. This is what he told us about Hezbollah in Lebanon and Hamas in Gaza:

"Hezbollah now [has] a tremendous base, and you can see that the international guarantees [promised by the U.N. after the 2006 war with Hezbollah in Lebanon] that were supposed to stop the flow of arms did nothing of the kind. And so now, instead of 4,000 rockets fired on the Galilee from that base, but we now have 40,000 rockets which are aimed at every part of Israel. And, at the same time, the same thing has happened in the south [the Gaza Strip]. We've had, by the way, a tremendous increase in the power of Hamas. It wasn't only politically strengthened, but very shortly afterwards, it militarily took over the Gaza Strip and kicked out the Palestinian Authority, and [the Gaza Strip] has become a base. [From Gaza] they've fired 4,000 rockets— that's the number since the unilateral disengagement—4,000."

Did you catch what Mr. Netanyahu just said? On the southern Lebanese border, Hezbollah now has 40,000 rockets aimed at every part of Israel. And further, we learned that Hamas was shooting rockets into Israel from Gaza at a rate of 16 to 18 times greater than ever before. Thus Israel was forced to go into Gaza in 2009 in an attempt to destroy all of the Hamas rockets.

Think for a moment: How would you feel if a neighboring nation was shooting rockets at where you live? One day, as we were taping at the border crossing between Israel and Gaza, a rocket went flying over our heads and exploded with a thunderous boom in Israel. I immediately thought, *How can this be happening? Why isn't the government doing something to stop that right now? How can they let rockets fly into Israeli territory day after day?* We were very motivated to raise these questions to various government leaders in our interviews.

We began with Major General Jacob Amidror, who for close to 28 years was the deputy military intelligence chief for the Israeli Defense Force. He recently retired and is now with the Jerusalem Center for Public Affairs. Listen to how he answered our questions about the rocket attacks:

"Many Israelis are very disappointed by the behavior of the Palestinians, who, you have to remember, were offered by Prime Minister Barak ninety percent of the West Bank and one hundred percent of

Gaza. The answer Israel received was war. Many Israelis have lost their hope that in our generation there will be a real peace between us and the Palestinians. And what we have to do [now] is to guarantee that until that day comes, we will be in a situation in which we can defend ourselves. And it may mean reconquering the West Bank, which we did in 2002. Maybe we will have to go back into Gaza [which Israel did shortly after this interview], because otherwise we are suffering every day mortars and rockets from Gaza into the populated Jewish areas around Gaza."

In other words, you don't have to spend a lot of time in Israel to realize how Israel is already being threatened and attacked on their borders by enemies in Lebanon, Syria, and Gaza. So where are things headed in the future? We believe you'll be surprised at the startling information God has revealed through the prophets about the nations that will come against Israel in the last days. Jimmy and I talked about this one day as we wound our way through the narrow streets of the Jewish Quarter in the Old City of Jerusalem. The streets were filled with the sights and sounds of children and shoppers, the smells of spices and perfumes, and carts of vegetables and fish.

"Jimmy, we're walking on this jam-packed street, and you couldn't have picked a more controversial piece of real estate in the world than where we're walking right now [the Jewish Quarter is not far from the Temple Mount]."

Enjoying every minute of the packed marketplace, he smiled and said, "That is exactly correct because ultimately, in the end times, there is going to be a battle between the Muslims and the Jews, and there is going to be a conflict that is going to end with the campaign of Armageddon, where all the armies of the world will gather around the city of Jerusalem. Now, this one square mile, comprising the Old City of Jerusalem, is going to be the main focus of Jesus Christ when He comes back to rebuild His temple on the Temple Mount here in this Old City. But the truth is, before that all happens, this place—this piece of real estate—is going to be a very controversial location, just as you said. It is going to intoxicate those who control it, according to the ancient Jewish prophet Zechariah."

I then said, "I've heard that those negotiating a peace treaty right now are talking about giving away this piece of real estate. They are talking about giving up the Jewish Quarter all the way up to the Temple Mount—the whole thing."

Jimmy agreed, "That is exactly right. They are now in negotiations, and we don't know where those negotiations are going to go, because the Jewish people and the Israeli government leaders do not want to give up the Temple Mount, though there has been some conversation that they may even consider that. But the negotiators at the table—the Palestinians and the Israelis—are talking about this. And the Palestinians argue that they are not going to give up a right to have this as their capital city in their Palestinian state. So we are going to continue to see the conflict unfold and intensify in the days ahead."

In the upcoming chapters, we will consider five issues related to this very conflict. First, we'll learn which nations are on the record as saying they want to destroy Israel. Second, we'll examine which nations the Bible predicts will come against Israel in the last days. Third, we'll tell you which nations Israel's *political* leaders see as a threat to Israel. Fourth, we'll find out which nations the Israeli and American *military* leaders believe are a threat to Israel. And fifth, we'll try to draw some conclusions from all we learn with the help of the Bible.

## The Nations Predicted in Prophecy

It was a beautiful, warm day with a clear blue sky overhead. We were taping on the Mount of Olives, looking across the Kidron Valley to the Temple Mount, where the Dome of the Rock was shining brightly in the sun. It was the perfect location for asking Jimmy to give an overview of the specific nations God reveals will try to capture and rule over the Temple Mount by destroying or subjugating the Jewish nation.

I started, "Jimmy, we are looking across the beautiful and majestic

Old City of Jerusalem and gazing on the Dome of the Rock and the al-Aqsa mosque, the third holiest site for the Islamic world. We are also viewing the Jewish Temple Mount here, which is sacred to the Jewish people across the world. So right in front of our eyes we see the most controversial piece of real estate in the world and two opposing sides. The prophets talked about what is to come. There is going to be a battle for Jerusalem. And this is what people really want to know: According to the Bible, which nations will play a role in the end-time scenario here in Israel?"

"You know, John, the Dome of the Rock speaks to the group of nations that will align against Israel because it is a Muslim building. Omar, a Muslim leader, built it on the Temple Mount in A.D. 691. It is the Islamic world that is going to come together and align themselves to try to destroy the Jewish state. There will be one exception in that group: Modern-day Russia is mentioned in Ezekiel 38."

Jimmy carefully opened his Bible and turned to Ezekiel chapter 38. "Here in Ezekiel 38 verse 2 we read about Gog of the land of Magog. Now, Gog would be the *person,* and Magog would be the *particular state* that Ezekiel is talking about. And according to biblical geography, Magog would have been that land mass north of the Caspian and Black Sea, which is Russia today.

"In the same verse Ezekiel also mentions Meshech and Tubal. Down in verse 6 he identifies Gomer and Togarmah. When traveling in Turkey recently I picked up an ancient Turkish map. In biblical times, Turkey was divided into four parts: Meshech, Tubal, Gomer, and Togarmah. So Ezekiel was talking about those who live in the areas we know as Russia and Turkey.

"Then in verse 5 he identifies Persia. Until 1936 there were three nations that comprised the area known as Persia: Afghanistan, Pakistan, and Iran. As you continue on in verse 5, Ezekiel identifies Ethiopia, or Cush in some Bible translations. That would likely include those today who live in Ethiopia, Somalia, and Sudan. Ezekiel also includes Libya, or in other Bible translations, Put. That's modern-day Libya.

"You have to coordinate these nations with Daniel 11:40-45. There, Daniel talks about 'the king of the North.' Earlier in chapter 11 you find out that 'the king of the North' is what we know as Syria today. Then Daniel identifies 'the king of the South,' which would be Egypt today.

"If you go over to the book of Psalms, in chapter 83, you will find another list of nations. Some scholars include these nations among those who will align themselves against Israel in the last days. Here, the Bible mentions the Ishmaelites—that's modern-day Saudi Arabia. Then in verse 7 it talks about Tyre; that's modern-day Lebanon. So the Bible gives us a list of nations, which today are Arab nations—with the exception of Russia—who will, according to Scripture, form this coalition to come against Israel in the last days."

I stopped Jimmy at this point to ask how he obtained his particular points of geography. I said, "The principle that you're using is that when the prophet identified a geographical area in his own day, he had no other option than to identify the area according to what the people of that day named it, right? The people living in those geographical areas were the ones whom God said would come against Israel in the future."

Jimmy explained, "John, I am using a hermeneutical [how to properly interpret a Bible passage] principle when I look at biblical geography. Who was the author writing about? For example, who was King David writing about when he wrote the Psalms? Who was Ezekiel writing about when he wrote Ezekiel 38? Who was Daniel writing about when he wrote Daniel chapter 11? These writers were talking about specific states or nations that were in existence at that time. We identify the nations today by the geographical regions back then. In order to accurately interpret Bible prophecy, we have to be specific about the locations the prophets were identifying in their own day."

I then asked, "You have lived in Israel since the early 1990s. Let's consider some of the countries in the Middle East, specifically those countries named in Bible prophecy. What do the latest intelligence

reports tell us about the movements and activities in the different countries?"

Jimmy started with Egypt. "In the south you have Egypt. Of course,
you also have the Gaza Strip, which is somewhat of a buffer between
Israel proper and Egypt itself. But when you look at Egypt, there within
Egypt you have the Islamic Brotherhood. They are the ones who birthed
the al Qaeda movement and Osama bin Laden. The number two man
in al Qaeda is from the Islamic Brotherhood. Yasser Arafat learned
everything he knew from a special sheikh (a high ranking Muslim
cleric) in the Islamic Brotherhood. Arafat organized the Palestinian
people and organized a fighting force that would spread throughout
the entire Gaza Strip. Hamas was founded by a blind sheikh named
Yassin. He comes directly from Egypt out of the Islamic Brotherhood.
So Israel faces threats from those in the Islamic Brotherhood who are
trying to control the Egyptian government today.

"Over to the east you have Jordan, which shares the longest border
with Israel [the Jordanian-Israeli border is 147 miles long]. Currently
we are not so much concerned about Jordan under the leadership of
King Abdullah. But what should be of concern is that seventy percent of the population of Jordan is Palestinian. And so, though King
Abdullah is from the Hashemite kingdom out of Saudi Arabia, he has
many Palestinian people and he is very much concerned about the peace
process. What will Israel decide about developing another Palestinian
state? Will that state extend over into Jordan? Though the borders are
pretty friendly, that long border goes from the south in Elat, Israel's
southernmost city, which is on the shores of the Red Sea, all the way
to Mount Hermon in the north. So Israel still has some concerns about
the large population of Palestinian people who live in Jordan.

"At the northeastern corner of Mount Hermon you have the border
with Syria. From that location we can look over the city of Kinetra
toward Damascus, about twenty-five to thirty miles to the northeast.
And there are reports that Syrian soldiers are being massed on that
border. Syria would like to take the Golan Heights from Israel. Now

when you travel up to Mount Hermon, you travel over the plateau of the Golan Heights to reach the foothills of Mount Hermon. That is a very fertile area Syria would dearly like to control. In fact, Syria has said it plans to get the Golan Heights back either diplomatically or militarily. So should Syria move into position on the Golan Heights, either by diplomacy or militarily, its presence will be a real threat to Israel.

"Across that northern border you also have Lebanon. Lebanon is in somewhat of a turmoil today. The leaders were not even able to elect a president for a number of months. But you have Hezbollah in southern Lebanon. Hezbollah are not Lebanese people; they are Iranians—they are part of the Iranian Revolutionary Guard sent into southern Lebanon by the Ayatollah Khomeini back in 1982. And today they are directed in everything that they do. Sheikh Nasrallah is the leader of Hezbollah. He gets his orders directly from Tehran and from President Ahmadinejad of Iran.

"And so there you have Egypt and Hamas in Gaza in the south. You have Jordan with a large Palestinian population on the eastern border. At the northeastern corner is Syria, which wants the Golan Heights back. In Lebanon you have Hezbollah, with forty thousand rockets aimed at Israel. This little State of Israel, just a little piece of real estate, is surrounded by these nations. Further out, there are twenty-three Arab nations with over three hundred million people surrounding Israel."

What is important to realize is that the nations mentioned in Bible prophecy are in many cases already aligned against Israel, preparing for future battles. In the next chapter, we'll look at the most alarming of these nations, the nation of Iran, and share what today's top Israeli political leaders are saying—words that frequently echo the Bible prophets of old.

# Chapter 6

# A Conflict Rekindled

Headlines across the world have reported that the State of Israel has sent more than 100 warplanes over the eastern Mediterranean on a training exercise to prepare for a long-distance strike against Iran.

In an interview with members of the Israeli government, we asked for an evaluation of the threat from Iran and the nations surrounding Israel. Who better to speak to than the current prime minister, Mr. Benjamin Netanyahu? He served as the prime minister of Israel from 1996–1999, was Israel's foreign minister in 2002–2003, and also served as Israel's ambassador to the United Nations from 1984–1988.

Netanyahu has once again become the prime minister of Israel at a crucial time. At a private briefing in April 2008, he quickly surveyed the recent events of the past that we are all familiar with. While we were taping our interview, he made some very serious statements:

"The militant Sunnis have bombed New York…Washington…other targets of al Qaeda from Bali to the European capitals." He paused for a moment, looked down, and in a clipped, deliberate manner, continued, "The militant Shiites in Iran are openly boasting that they are racing to develop nuclear weapons with the explicit announced goal of wiping Israel from the face of the earth and re-establishing the caliphate—of course, under militant Shiite Iranian rule. The caliphate includes the territories from Iran to Spain. [In the process, they are] developing long-range ballistic missiles first that are targeted to every European capital and within a decade to reach the eastern coast of the American mainland."

We were somewhat surprised at Mr. Netanyahu's forceful words. But during other interviews in the weeks to come, we learned that virtually all of Israel's leaders view Iran the same way. For example, one afternoon we sat down with Moshe Arens, former Israeli ambassador to the United States and former Israeli minister of defense for three different administrations.

I (Jimmy) asked Moshe Arens, "According to the Israeli intelligence community, Iran is the number one threat to the Jewish State of Israel. Would you agree with that assessment?"

"Well, that's correct because Iran…unlike terrorist organizations… [is] the only state in the region—as a matter of fact, the only state in the world—whose prime minister, Ahmadinejad, openly threatens Israel and says Israel has to be wiped off the map. So here you have a declared enemy. Now, Iran is not a minuscule state, and the Iranians are [determined to acquire] nuclear weapons. So when somebody is talking and working towards nuclear capability, and tells you that you need to be wiped off the face of the earth, it's a real threat."

Turning to another military leader, we talked with Major General Jacob Amidror. He was formerly the deputy military intelligence chief for the Israeli Defense Force. In 1995, he was the representative who visited American officials to convince them that Iran was a rising and dangerous nuclear power. The "smoking gun" that led to action against Iran was evidence found on an Iranian laptop computer that outlined Tehran's nuclear activities. We asked him if he agreed with others that Iran is *the* major threat to Israel.

Amidror responded, "Yes. Today, there is no question that Iran is the main threat to the State of Israel. First of all, Iran is going to be nuclear if [others won't stop it]. And from the Iranian point of view it's not that Israel is the only enemy, but it symbolizes the evil of the world. And [there's] no question [that a] nuclear Iran is a threat to the liberal democratic world and Israel symbolizing it in the Middle East. So we are under threat from Iran in this area."

Another powerful Israeli government leader is the current speaker of the Knesset, Mr. Reuven Rivlin, who is also a member of the Likud party. The speaker of the Knesset is a similarly powerful position as the U.S. speaker of the House.

We asked Mr. Rivlin, "In this Knesset building there has been discussion about the possibility of a preemptive attack on Iran. Conversation has taken place between the United States and Israel about such an attack. Do you think that would happen, and could it happen, or does it need to happen?"

Rivlin replied, "If no one will take [action] and Israel will have to take [action] on its own, we will have to consider and evaluate what we have to do. And there are possibilities for Israel. But the Iran problem is not the problem of Israel; it is the problem of the free world. It is the problem of Europe, and they have to realize it. I really believe that Iran should be taken care of by the entire family of nations, not only by Israel. Israel has to take care and to know that once [it has] to face the threat of being destroyed by a possible nuclear weapon from the side of Iran, they will have to do [something], and we know what we have to do."

## Iran Mentioned by the Old Testament Prophets

After talking with these political leaders, Jimmy and I discussed the biblical significance of the words from these top-ranking Israelis as we sat in the Knesset auditorium overlooking the speaker's platform [for the sake of clarity, I (John) will be interviewing Jimmy in this section].

I shared, "We've just finished talking with the former speaker of the Knesset, and he said Iran is a real threat. Further, the Israeli government that meets in this room is going to have to deal with it. It's interesting to me that what we are hearing all ties in to biblical prophecy as well."

Jimmy explained in detail, "It certainly does. Ezekiel 38:5 mentions Persia. And until 1936, Persia was the name of three countries that we know today as Iran, Afghanistan, and Pakistan. So the Bible says Iran will be a major player in end-time prophecy. And it is at that time that not only Iran, but also Turkey, Saudi Arabia, Lebanon, Afghanistan, Iran, and Pakistan will be involved. You're also talking about Somalia, Ethiopia, and Sudan. These nations, led by Russia, will come into this region to try to destroy the Jewish state."

As we stood in silence and looked at the people wandering in and out of the Knesset auditorium, I couldn't help but think of Benjamin Netanyahu's solemn remarks when we asked him, "Is there widespread agreement on Iran?" Netanyahu spoke slowly and clearly of the total unanimity that Israel's government leaders have for dealing with Iran's threat. He said:

"I think we have to do everything in our power to prevent the arming of Iran with nuclear weapons. On this, I have to say, there is absolute unanimity in Israel. There's no opposition, there is no coalition, not only on the declaratory level but on every other level. There are no party lines on this and there are no party divisions on this...I think this is a growing consensus. It wasn't always the case. The clarity of this threat wasn't always understood, but it is understood now and we have absolute unanimity on this. And I can say that in some of the leading governments in the world right now, there is equally a growing consensus."

## An American Military Leader's Warnings About Iran

We also wanted to find out how some of our American military leaders assessed the situation between Israel and Iran. One of the people we interviewed was retired American three-star Lieutenant General William G. Boykin, a veteran of the Army's top-secret Delta Force. He has served as Commanding General at the U.S. Army Special Forces Command at Fort Bragg, North Carolina and Commanding General at the U.S. Army John F. Kennedy Special Warfare Center. He was assigned to the Office of the Joint Chiefs of Staff at the Pentagon as Chief Special Operations Division, and some time afterward, he served at the CIA as deputy director of special activities. He was promoted to the rank of Lieutenant General in 2003. Later, he became deputy undersecretary of defense for intelligence; then he retired in 2007. We had the privilege of interviewing him while in Israel, and we asked for his thoughts about Iran.

I (John) remember meeting him. He literally towered over me and was a powerful man. I welcomed him and patted him on the back. I felt like I was hitting iron. After we sat down on a wide veranda overlooking the Kidron Valley and the magnificent Temple Mount, we began our interview.

I said, "I would like to ask for your assessment of the different nations surrounding Israel and the situation the world faces in this regard. We've talked to members of the Knesset, academic leaders, and military leaders, and they all agree that Iran is Israel's number one threat. From the American side, when you were deputy undersecretary of defense for intelligence, how did you evaluate Iran? What is the world facing right now? What is Israel facing?"

Boykin paused before responding. "Well, I agree with those Israelis who have told you they fear Iran as their number one threat. I think that it is. I think Iran is the number one threat probably to the whole world. A lot of people don't take Ahmadinejad seriously. But all you have to do is study his background a little bit, and you realize that this guy has been a [fanatical] zealot since he was a very young child. He truly believes that it is his personal responsibility to usher in the *Mahdi,* or the Islamic messiah.

"And if you go back and look at some of the early Islamic writings, you will find that many like Ahmadinejad believe that [the *Mahdi* will return] in a period of chaos and bloodshed...Many of them also believe that the caliphate [one sole authority and leader in Islam] has to be re-established. Ahmadinejad believes that what he has been called by Allah to do is to create that chaos and that bloodshed to bring the *Mahdi* to earth. [Combine that theology] with the fact that he began a number of years ago to develop a nuclear capability. And just yesterday he announced that he now has over six thousand centrifuges,[4] which is probably double what he needs for peaceful purposes. And…he believes that if he could destroy Israel in obedience to Allah—even if it meant a retaliatory strike by the Israelis that killed millions of Iranians—he is very comfortable with that because Jews and Israel are the infidels—[he and] his people, who are followers of Allah, [will] go to heaven."

## Is Iran Developing Nuclear Weapons?

Everyone we interviewed mentioned that Iran was developing nuclear weapons. We wanted to know when they believed that dreadful moment of success would occur. Now, remember, in this section of *Israel Under Fire* we are considering five things: First, the nations today who want to destroy Israel; second, the nations the Bible predicts will come against Israel in the last days; third, the nations Israeli political leaders see as a threat to Israel; fourth, the nations Israeli and American military leaders believe are a threat to Israel; and fifth, the conclusions we should draw from all that. In governments across the world, the most important question being asked is this: When will Iran have enough enriched uranium to make a nuclear bomb? When we were with Mr. Netanyahu, he made this statement:

"Our intelligence chiefs have publicly said that it would take Iran three years to develop the critical knowledge to produce a weapon. Well, there are now about two years left; they haven't changed (as far as I know) their assessment. So this is a problem that we all face."

But as you will hear, Israel's timetable of when Iran will develop a nuclear weapon has shortened. The former head of the Mossad (Institute for Intelligence and Special Operations), Shabtai Shavit, said that

Israel has just 12 months in which to destroy Iran's nuclear program or risk coming under nuclear attack itself. He warned that time was running out for preventing Iran's leaders from getting a bomb.

At the same time that Shabtai Shavit made his statement in the United States, a Pentagon official identified two "red lines" that could trigger such an Israeli attack. These red lines refer to this principle: "If you dare cross this line, Israel will take action." The first line would be when Iran's nuclear facility at Natanz produces enough highly enriched uranium to make a nuclear weapon—something that, according to U.S. and Israeli assessments, could happen in 2009. "The red line would be crossed not when Iran gets to that point, but *before* [it gets] to that point," the official said. "So, we are now in the window of vulnerability."[5] In other words, Israel is not going to wait for someone to develop a weapon and have it ready to launch before Israel takes action. Israel is determined to keep Iran from obtaining a nuclear weapon in the first place.

He said that the second red line would be crossed when Iran acquires SA-20 air defense missile systems from Russia. Israel would want to make its attack before these sophisticated defensive weapons are in place, because the defensive weapons would make Israel's air attack much more difficult.

In our interview with Lieutenant General Boykin, we asked, "If neither the European Union nor the United States will join Israel in a strike against Iran, won't Israel be forced into a corner and have to defend itself?"

He responded, "John, that's the same situation that Golda Meir faced once. She had to strike the Egyptian air force because she knew that the threat was imminent. They were going to attack Israel. And I think the leadership of Israel at some point is going to come to that same point with Iran if things don't change between now and then. Every country has the right of self-defense. Self-defense does not mean necessarily waiting until you're attacked before fighting back. And in Israel's case, they may come to that point if nobody else is going to help them.

"They know that Ahmadinejad has already declared repeatedly that his objective is to destroy Israel—to wipe it off the face of the map, to use his words. I think Israel will come to the point where it's going to have to make that decision even if no one else will help."

As speculation in the world grows that Israel is contemplating air strikes against Iran, General Mohammed Ali Jafari, the chief of Iran's feared Revolutionary Guards, declared that a pre-emptive strike against Iran by Israel might prompt a wave of Iranian retaliatory attacks against both Israeli and U.S. targets. He said if Iran came under attack, it might hit the Jewish state with missiles and block the Gulf of Hormuz to stop gulf oil exports. He went on to say that Israel is completely within the range of the Islamic republic's missiles, and that the strait between Iran and Oman is a vital conduit for energy supplies for many nations, with as much as 40 percent of the world's crude passing through that point.

Iran then initiated further steps to retaliate against Israel by moving ballistic missiles into launch positions that target various sites in Israel, including the Dimona nuclear plant, where Israel's own nuclear weapons are believed to be made. This prompted Binyamin Ben-Eliezer, Israel's minister for national infrastructure, to warn that "Iran will be wiped off the face of the earth if it dares to fire any missile at us."[6]

Shaul Mofaz, former Israeli chief of staff and defense minister, added, "Other options are disappearing. The [U.N.] sanctions are not effective. There will be no choice but to attack Iran to halt the Iranian nuclear program. Iran's President Mahmoud Ahmadinejad will disappear before Israel does."[7]

In light of these escalating threats and actions, how do the leading intelligence agencies of the world assess the Iranian threat? Benjamin Netanyahu laid it out before us very succinctly:

"We have our own view of what Iran is doing. I must tell you...in all honesty I think there is widespread agreement among the leading intelligence agencies of the world (of the Western world, at least—I'm not sure if I would limit it to the Western world)—that Iran is galloping to develop nuclear weapons. Ahmadinejad a few days ago went on a grand tour celebrating another six thousand centrifuges. What is he developing? What does he have those centrifuges for? They are building ballistic missiles that have only one use...When Iran has the second largest or third largest oil reserves in the world, you know that their energy problem is not uppermost in their minds, right?...My purpose here is to try to draw attention to the fact that if we [the world] do not act, time is not on our side. It's on the other side."

After our interview with Benjamin Netanyahu, we reflected on his words: "If we do not act, time is not on our side. It's on the other side." We were on the streets of Jerusalem when we heard the Muslim call to prayer in the background. Five times every day, observant Muslims must pray. The Muslim presence, territory, and rocket attacks reminded us of the imminent threat that the Jewish people face today. If the Islamic world is the lowest common denominator among the nations that are going to gather themselves against the Jewish people, then the number one threat today would be Iran. And that threat is not the only one the Jewish people will have to face. They'll have to face other nations that surround them in the Middle East—Syria, Egypt, Libya, Turkey, Iran, Afghanistan, Pakistan, Somalia, Ethiopia, and Sudan. According to the biblical prophets, these nations will gather together and come against the Jewish state. As we listened to that Islamic call to prayer, we thought about the battles yet ahead for the Jewish people and the nation of Israel and the prime minister's statement: "Time is not on our side."

Chapter 7

# A THREAT REASSESSED

The facts we presented in the last chapter about Iran are well-known to world leaders, and fears of a possible Israeli military attack on Iran's nuclear facilities are growing. People are fearful of the looming consequences. Everyone realizes that if Iran launches a counterattack on Israel and disrupts the flow of oil from the Middle East, the whole world will be affected. Many Christians and Jews are asking, "Didn't Ezekiel 38 predict a future war in which Israel will fight many of the nations in the Middle East? Are any of the nations named by Ezekiel the same ones making threats against Israel today?" In this chapter, we'll closely examine the fascinating prophecies God uttered to this prophet. And we will talk with military leaders in Israel who comment on the very things we read about in Ezekiel 38.

Which nations did Ezekiel prophesy would align against Israel in the last days? Here are the ancient nations and their modern equivalents:

- *Gog in the land of Magog* (verse 2). Magog was the area north of the Caspian and Black Seas, part of modern-day Russia. Gog refers to the leader of this land.

- *Meshech, Tubal, Gomer, Togarmah* (verses 2,6). These refer to parts of modern-day Turkey.

- *Persia* (verse 5). This ancient nation included the territory now occupied by Afghanistan, Pakistan, and Iran.
- *Ethiopia/Cush* (verse 5). This could include Ethiopia, Somalia, and Sudan.
- *Libya* (verse 5). This refers to modern-day Libya and possibly other areas west of Libya.

In addition to the nations in Ezekiel 38, we need to include those mentioned in Daniel 11:40-45:

- *The King of the North.* This refers to the area of modern-day Syria.
- *The King of the South.* This refers to the area of modern-day Egypt.

Some scholars also include Psalm 83 as referring to unfulfilled prophecy. If so, this would include:

- *The Ishmaelites* (verse 6) used to live in what is now Saudi Arabia.
- *Tyre* (verse 5). This refers to modern-day Lebanon.

After reviewing what Ezekiel 38, Daniel 11, and Psalm 83 record, do we see military pacts and agreements shaping up between these nations? Could they form the military coalition that Ezekiel said would come against Israel?

In our visits with Israel's political and military leaders, we asked about the threats Israel is facing from these nations in the Middle East. Benjamin Netanyahu forcefully described the threats Israel is currently facing from Iran,

Syria, Lebanon, and the Palestinians—some of the very same nations Ezekiel wrote about. Here is what he believes is currently taking place in the Middle East. His words are riveting:

"If you look at what has happened…not economically…but politically to the world—what has happened in terms of politics and security in the decades that have passed, you see a clear trajectory of the rise of militant Islam. You see it not only taking over countries (which it has) but [it's] also extending its sway over many people [as the population of Muslims continues to grow exponentially].

"Obviously there are two strains in this dogma: the militant Sunnis and the militant Shiites…burst out in Iran…A decade later, the victory of the Mujahedin heralded the rise of al Qaeda.

"Obviously they haven't been able to take over the majority. And even the minority is small, but the minority of a very, very large majority is troubling [just 10 percent of 1.5 billion Muslims is 150 million people]. But their goals are unlimited. Whatever their successes so far, they don't intend to stop. They continue [and have] been competing with each other: Who will produce the…more spectacular successes for the creed?

"And in the process, they've rolled over, from Iran, they've rolled over, they're clearly meddling in Iran, the congressional testimony last week described this. They have already more than meddled in Lebanon with the Hezbollah there now. It used to be said Hezbollah is a state within a state. It's not clear that has not been reversed, given that Hezbollah has now some forty thousand rockets, which is a lot more than they had before the second Lebanon War. There are much more lethal rockets—long-range rockets that can reach a good portion of this country. And, this is all done by Iran. It cannot be understood as anything but an Iranian operation. They've already taken over half of Palestinian society; they've taken over Gaza, and they're agitating to take more. So, this is not merely a local problem. This is a global problem. Obviously, if Iran acquires nuclear weapons, everything that we've been talking about will pale in comparison."

## Enemies on All Sides

When we visited the office of Major General Jacob Amidror, the former deputy military intelligence chief for the Israeli Defense Force, he told us that today Israel is facing a four-pronged attack coming from Iran, Syria, Lebanon, and the Palestinians.

He noted, "Today, there can be no question that Iran is the main threat to the State of Israel. And there are some dangerous phases to this threat. First…Iran is going to be nuclear if it will not be stopped by others.

"The second phase is connected to the fact that Iran is ready to invest a lot of money, a lot of efforts, even to risk its people by sending them to build Hezbollah in the north and Hamas in the south. And there are two extensions of Iran around Israel, one in Gaza and one in Lebanon. And together under the umbrella of nuclear Iran, it will be easier for both the Iranian extension in Lebanon and the Iranian extension in Gaza to act against Israel.

"The third phase of this threat is the relation between Syria and Iran. The Iranians are helping the Syrians to build their military forces, helping them with money, and by having very good relations in the area of research and development, mainly of rockets and so on. And [there is] no question nuclear Iran is a threat to the liberal democratic world and Israel, which symbolizes it in the Middle East. So we are under threat from Iran in these areas."

Another Israeli leader that we interviewed was former Israeli defense minister Mr. Moshe Arens. We asked if he thought Israel should make a move against Iran before it becomes nuclear capable."

Arens carefully noted, "Well, as has been so frequently said by Israeli spokesmen, our prime minister, and [former] President Bush in the United States, nuclear capability in the hands of the Iranians is not only a threat against Israel—it's a threat to the world. And so we are hoping that the world (or the community of nations led by the United States) will take appropriate measures, whether they're economic sanctions or maybe some other things [to ensure that Iran never reaches] nuclear capability. That would be a bad thing, [and] not just for Israel."

I then posed the most difficult question regarding Iran's potential nuclear development: "If Iran could achieve its goal of building a nuclear weapon of mass destruction, do you think Israel would either try to delay the development of that weapon or eliminate it altogether?"

Arens did not hesitate in his response, but he guarded how much he would share. "The horizon for [Iran] reaching that capability at the rate they're going is not infinite. It's not far off. [As for] what Israel would or should do, I don't think it would be appropriate for me to talk about that in public. That's something that needs to be discussed and decided at the appropriate level...by the people who carry the direct responsibility for Israel's security today. And I did that in the past, but I don't carry that responsibility today."

## American Military Leaders on Potential Threats to Israel

How do some of our American military leaders assess the situation in the Middle East? To answer this question, we turned to Lieutenant General William G. Boykin, who was the United States undersecretary of defense for intelligence. Here is what he had to say:

"Iran has clearly established linkages to Hezbollah. I think...in the summer of 2006 (I don't think there's any question, not in my mind at least) that Iran orchestrated the two-front attack on Israel. Iran supported both Hamas and Hezbollah. Iran is arming Hezbollah in south Lebanon. Iran even paid the families of people in Lebanon who lost family members during the 2006 conflict there. So Iran is [very closely] tied to the terrorist groups there."

Transitioning to other nations, I turned to Israel's northeastern neighbor, Syria, asking, "How would you analyze what's going on in Syria, and where does it rank militarily?"

He answered, "Well, the Syrians...have a capable military. It's certainly not as strong as Iran…Syria has continued to give safe haven and support to Hezbollah. I also think that Assad, the president of Syria, has continued his father's desire to have the Golan Heights back that was lost to the Israelis. It has become a personal thing with Assad, and I think he wants the Golan back. And that will always be problematic in terms of a reason for Syria to attack Israel."

We then asked about Turkey. Boykin noted, "NATO [the North Atlantic Treaty Organization] has a base in Turkey… The United States has been close friends with Turkey, and Turkey has even applied for membership in the European Union. At the same time, the European Union is now kind of backing away from that. And there's another more radical faction that's coming up in Turkey."

I then asked Boykin to evaluate the importance of Turkey to the Middle East.

"I think Turkey is strategic and I think this is one of the really difficult issues for NATO. Because on the one hand, we have a NATO alliance and Turkey has always been a member of that. On the other hand, we have the European Union arising, and countries like Germany have refused to allow Turkey to join the European Union. The fear is that refusal may drive them toward the Islamic camp, to where they become—rather than the secular state that they have been for decades—an Islamic Republic. This would fracture NATO and create another problem in the Middle East and probably throw the balance of power in the Middle East way out of kilter."

Turning to Russia, the land covered by the prophet Ezekiel as the land of Magog, I asked Boykin, "Former president Putin of Russia has been involved in many of these countries—with Sudan, Iran, Syria, and others. What do you believe his new involvements are all about?"

"That's a good question. You know, I think what we're going to see is [Putin as] the next czar in Russia. I mean, many experts will tell you he is the most powerful ruler of Russia over the last one hundred years. What are his objectives? Well, I think they're multiple. Number one, I think that he needs warm water ports. He needs to move large reserves of oil. He needs pipelines. And he needs allies in the Middle East and the Gulf. And I think that's what he has been working toward."

Fascinated by Lieutenant General Boykin's assessments, we then asked, "Part of your official job as deputy undersecretary for defense was to analyze counterterrorism. How should America counter some of the attacks that may happen in the future? How can we protect against the supply of oil being cut off in the Middle East? What kind of crisis might we face?"

Boykin answered, "Very soon, America will be importing about sixty percent of its oil requirements. And then you look at the Gulf and [consider that] it holds fifty-eight to sixty percent of the known reserves in the world today. And we're dependent upon that. I think we have a huge problem. Now, the Gulf countries have continued that supply of oil. But the fact of the matter is, they could cut it off. Or they could jack the prices up so high that it would destroy our economy."

## Oil and a Nuclear Iran—a World Problem

During an interview, Israeli prime minister Benjamin Netanyahu tied oil and nuclear Iran together as a world problem. He said, "The potential shortage of oil isn't the only problem the world faces. If Iran acquires nuclear weapons, everything that we've been talking about will pale in comparison. Because that power would allow them to extend power, threaten, realize the threats, and make good on their threats, and [all of this] would be on a level that we have not [yet] seen, nor one that we can readily imagine. It will put the oil reserves of the Gulf under their sway. They could easily bring down governments or fold them into their realm. They will inspire and encourage the radicals in the various Islamic communities that they are targeting around the world. And they will, in turn, be inspired by the fact that…the acquisition of nuclear weapons is a providential sign of the coming victory of the true believers. And, of course, they might make good on their twisted ideas of ending Zionism and extending their realm by other means. So this is a threat to the entire world, and it cannot be seen as anything but that."

Iran may serve as the major current threat to Israel, but it is not the only one. Many of the nations around Israel also desire their destruction and could be motivated by Iran's radical leadership to move forward to hasten their cause.

So, you have heard from some of Israel's political and military leaders and an American general who analyzed intelligence and made plans for counterterrorism.

How does what they say mirror what the prophets say is coming in the future? During every major crisis in the Middle East, Christians and non-Christians, secular magazines such as *Time* and *Newsweek*, and even media outlets such as CNN, ABC, NBC, CBS, and FOX (somewhere along the line) make reference to what the Bible says about a coming worldwide conflict in the Middle East. As we have traveled, people have asked the same questions: "Doesn't the Bible say something about what is going on in the world? Doesn't it talk about the end times and a final worldwide battle called Armageddon? Do you think something like that could really happen?"

We will begin to unfold some of the surprising answers to these questions in our next chapter.

Chapter 8

# A BATTLE REANALYZED

W hat tragic events would happen to us, our world, oil, the economy, or our health, if the unthinkable happened—that is, if
a nuclear exchange took place between Iran and Israel or a bomb went
off in some major capital city? Israel and Iran are highlighted in world
news nearly every day. The fears of a possible Israeli military strike on
Iran's nuclear facilities are growing. Yet many Americans assume that
because Israel is so far away, whatever happens there doesn't matter to
us here in the United States. Well, they are wrong. The world today is
very interconnected. What takes place in one area can severely affect
another.

In this chapter, we will look at how events in the Middle East
can have a profound impact worldwide. We will take you to the four
borders of Israel, including stops at the Golan Heights, the Sea of Galilee, and the Jordan River Valley and recount some of the past battles
fought in Israel and Israel's relations with its neighbors. We will also
discuss the potential military nightmare that would occur if a nuclear
exchange took place between Iran and Israel in the near future. Did
you know military analysts in America and elsewhere have already
published reports of how many people could die in such an exchange,
and what could happen to world oil supplies? Finally, we will draw

some conclusions as to where we are in history according to what God has revealed in Bible prophecy.

## Beyond Israel's Borders

We had just traveled with our film crew to an area about 45 minutes outside of Jerusalem down toward the Dead Sea. Jimmy and I had been discussing Iran and some of Israel's other neighbors. Jimmy, who was driving the Land Rover, suddenly pulled off the highway and took us toward some sand dunes and a stretch of palm trees. The sky was clear blue and the temperature was 87 degrees. When we stopped on the top of a sand dune, we got out and walked up a little hill that gave us a panoramic view of the landscape around us.

Jimmy began, "John, there are four countries whose borders surround Israel. The longest border is with Jordan. [Also,] you have Syria and Lebanon to the north, and you have Egypt to the south. These nations will play, according to Bible prophecy, a key role in attacking Israel. Even today as we talk, there are reports that Syrian troops are massing on the border right near the Golan Heights. What's more, you have a very volatile situation as far as the Gaza Strip is concerned.

"Let's continue onward; I want to show you some very interesting areas related to our discussion." We climbed back into the Land Rover and began our journey across Israel. It was about nine o'clock in the morning.

Our adventure started to concern me when Jimmy said, "Now, just up here on the road I am going to turn off to the left and we will go off the beaten path. Don't worry about the sign there that says 'Danger: Land Mines.'"

"Thanks a lot," I responded as we headed up a steep mountain road.

"That is the Jordan Valley down below. The southern end the Sea of Galilee will come into view in just a moment." When it did, it was a beautiful, shimmering blue body of water surrounded by lush green fields. But here we only spotted the southern tip of the sea. We drove almost all the way to the top of a mountain, got out of the Land Rover, and walked the rest of the way to the top. As we came around a bend, Jimmy said, "From here we can see the Jordan Valley. As we come around, we'll walk up onto a bunker that dates back to the 1967 Six-Day War. From there we can see the mountains of Gilead, one of the mountain ranges that run down the Jordan Valley. Up here, we're in the foothills of the Golan Heights."

Turning to an abandoned bunker, Jimmy then said, "John, this bunker dates back to June 1, 1967, the time of the Six-Day War. Israel was under attack from Jordan in the east, which you can see right across there, represented by the mountains of Gilead. From the north came the Syrians, who also wanted to destroy the Jewish nation. And, in fact, Syria was encamped right at this place on the Golan Heights. Look out upon the Sea of Galilee, and you can see how this spot gave the military advantage to the Syrians in their attempts to destroy the Jewish nation and the fertile valley below." As we looked out across the mountainous terrain, we could see for miles. We could see the farmers in their tractors, workers in their fields, and in the far distance, boats on the Sea of Galilee.

Jimmy continued, "Egypt attacked Israel from the south. So from every direction there were enemies attacking the Jewish state. What is almost miraculous is that in six days the Israelis were able to push back the Egyptians. They basically wiped out their air force. They were able to push back the Jordanians and Syrians and set up these buffer zones. This is a very fertile valley; and it's a valley that all nations would like to have. At this time, Israel has it."

## The Controversial Golan Heights

We returned to the Land Rover, and we continued our mountainous climb to the top of the disputed Golan Heights in northern Israel. The journey took us on a well-worn dusty road that soon transitioned into a two-lane paved road with hairpin turns climbing high up the mountain. After about 30 minutes of driving across this elevated terrain, we came to a beautiful plateau leading to a high cliff and breathtaking view.

"I bring people here because I want them to understand how strategic this piece of geography is. It's the Golan Heights. We're now directly above the Sea of Galilee which is fourteen miles long and seven miles wide. You can see the city of Tiberias over there. It's a major tourist area." We gazed out on the crystal blue lake and could see the reflections of towns and cities along the water's shoreline.

"This is also the major water source, John, for the entire State of Israel. And if indeed somebody were to control this spot, they could shut the water off for the Israeli people. You could see what is at stake here. Only one president of the United States has ever come up here, and only one secretary of state. And yet America, the European Union, and the United Nations have at varying points in history made decisions trying to force the Jewish state to give away this valuable and strategic piece of property."

After returning to the Land Rover, we drove along to the Syrian border, and then to Israel's border with Lebanon, and ended up at the border crossing at Gaza next to the Mediterranean. As we drove back to Jerusalem at night, the points about how small Israel is, and how close its enemies are, were very apparent.

During our journey, we were impressed with the beauty of Israel. All in one day, we drove on desert sands, passed through lush green valleys, navigated high snow-capped mountains, and experienced the tropical heat of Tel Aviv. When we returned to the worn streets of the Old City of Jerusalem, we once again returned to the subject of what the Bible says this beautiful country will face in the days ahead, as well as where the attacks will come from.

Jimmy observed, "You know, John, as we walk among the Palestinian community here in the Old City of Jerusalem in the Arab Quarter, I am reminded that there is going to be a conflict. It's one that has been going on for four thousand years. It started with Jacob and Esau, in Genesis 25. You can trace it throughout the entire Bible and see how this conflict continues even today. This age-old conflict is still the major focus of the world. All the terrorist leaders say the problem in the Middle East is that the Israelis will not give back to the Palestinians the land that is rightfully theirs."

Jimmy continued as we turned a corner into a crowded area of people, shops, and vendors. "Now, this is a piece of real estate, this area of the Old City of Jerusalem, including the Temple Mount, that the Palestinians claim is theirs. Well, there is going to be a continuing conflict over this, and the Bible tells us in the book of Obadiah that ultimately, when the Messiah, Jesus Christ, comes back, that's when the conflict will be completed. In fact, Obadiah says the Jews will be the fire, the wood that is burning. And the Edomites, the descendants of Esau, the Palestinians, will be the stubble in that fire. They will be burned up and they will cease to exist again in history. John, right now, we are walking right in the middle of the area that is going to be at the center of this battle."

## The Muslim End-Times Scenario

Some people are surprised when they find out that Muslims believe in the end times. However, what Muslims believe will happen is vastly different from the scenario presented in the Bible. I brought up this issue with Jimmy: "I find it interesting that Muslims are looking for a Messiah as well, except it's not Jesus."

"Of course," Jimmy agreed, "they are looking for the *Mahdi,* the Islamic Messiah. Everybody must realize that eschatology [teachings about the final days of world history] is not only part of Jewish, or Christian theology; the Muslim world has an eschatology all their own. They believe their Messiah, the *Mahdi,* is coming. And in fact, more and more Islamic literature is pointing to the city of Jerusalem as the location where the Muslim Messiah will rule over a worldwide caliphate. They believe that an Islamic kingdom, under the leadership of Allah, will be set up by the Muslim Messiah and headquartered right on the Temple Mount here in the Old City of Jerusalem." But do we see signs of Islamic theology and eschatology driving events in the Middle East?

During our travels in Israel, each day we read the latest news headlines in Jerusalem. Every day there was at least one mention of the Iranian threat. Many days, this was on the front page of the newspaper. As we walked through the Knesset building to tape some of our interviews, we couldn't help but notice some of the photographs of famous world leaders who had come to address the Knesset, including President Anwar Sadat of Egypt, and many European and American leaders. There were also pictures of Israel's leaders at the U.N., and of course, pictures of Israeli cabinet meetings during times of war. The headlines in the news and the historical photos brought us back to the current threat from Iran and how it could affect the countries surrounding Israel. As we stood overlooking the Knesset auditorium, I mentioned to Jimmy, "What does Bible prophecy say Israel and the leaders who meet here will face in the days ahead?"

Jimmy answered, "Well, I can tell you this: Benjamin Netanyahu has stood there at that podium and addressed this Knesset and said, 'Iran is the number one threat. We have returned to the days of World War II and the Nazi regime of Adolf Hitler.' He was referring to President Ahmadinejad of Iran. Israeli intelligence warns that Iran is the nation's number one threat. Of course they were speaking about the Iranian military buildup as well as the possibility of a nuclear weapon of mass destruction being used as a warhead on one of the long-range missiles Iran has developed. In fact, President Ahmadinejad said he has 1600 missiles that can hit any spot in the State of Israel. So Iran is the number one threat."

Later, when we interviewed Netanyahu, he shared much more on this issue: "I said a year and a half ago that the year is 1938 and Iran is Germany, and it's racing to acquire nuclear weapons. Well, if that's the case, then we're in 1939. Our intelligence chiefs have publicly said that it would take Iran three years to develop the critical knowledge to produce a weapon. Well, there are now about two years left." Netanyahu said that in 2008. A month after our interview with Netanyahu, the former head of the Mossad said there were only 12 months left before Iran would have a nuclear bomb. Either way, the clock is ticking, and time is running out.

Netanyahu then said to Jimmy, "You asked me about comparisons [of Ahmadinejad] with Hitler. Well, let me give you one comparison. There are obviously differences. One is advancing the supremacy of race; the other is advancing the supremacy of creed. These are different societies, different histories. But the use of unbridled power, the physical elimination of enemies, that takes place all the time—all the time.

"I'm not sure the world press is fully aware of what is happening inside Iran and how enemies are simply being dispatched; I mean, killed, murdered all the time and publicly, too. Publicly, and not only quietly. This is taking place all the time in Iran. And a small sect imposes its will with violent means on the society at large for the purpose of outward aggression. There are these similarities.

"Here's a dissimilarity with Hitler and Germany: whereas in the previous case Hitler embarked on a global conflict *before* developing nuclear weapons, this regime is first developing nuclear weapons before it embarks on a global conflict. Now, you know, if the Middle East turns into a nuclear powder keg, that's very, very bad. I mean, we really don't want that happening in our world."

## Economic Armageddon and the Potential Death Toll in the Middle East

What would happen if Iran does develop a nuclear weapon, and a nuclear exchange with Israel occurs? Anthony Cordesman, an American national security analyst who has also served as a director of intelligence assessment in the office of the U.S. Secretary of Defense, has written, "If Tehran gets the bomb and a nuclear exchange with Israel occurs, some 16 million to 28 million Iranians would be dead within 21 days, and between 200,000 to 800,000 Israelis would die. Jordan would also suffer severe radiation damage from an Iranian strike on Tel Aviv." [8] He estimates that "it is theoretically possible that the Israeli state, economy and organized society might just survive, but Iran would not survive as an organized society." [9]

Further, Cordesman expects that Israel would need to keep a reserve strike capability to ensure no other power can capitalize on the Iranian strike. Such a reserve might target key Arab neighbors such as Syria, Egypt, and the Persian Gulf states. He goes on to describe the potential horrific outcome: "A full-scale Israeli attack on Syria would kill up to 18 million people within 21 days, and a Syrian recovery would not be possible. At the same time, a Syrian attack on Israel with all of its chemical and biological warfare assets could kill up to 800,000 Israelis. But," he says, "Israeli society would still recover."

What if there's an Israeli attack on Egypt? Cordesman does not give a death toll here, but believes it would certainly be in the tens of millions. He does say, "It would mean the end of Egypt as a functioning society." Further, Cordesman says we must recognize that "the oil wells, refineries and ports along the Gulf would also be targets in the event of a mass nuclear response by an Israel convinced that it was being dealt a potentially mortal blow." The resulting nuclear contamination would mean the permanent loss of oil from the Middle East.

Cordesman sums it up this way: "Being contained within the region, such a nuclear exchange might not be Armageddon for the human race; but it would certainly be Armageddon for the global economy." Martin Walker of United Press International has stated, "Anthony Cordesman's analysis spells out the end of Persian civilization, quite probably the end of Egyptian civilization, and the end of the Oil Age."

## Where God Says History Is Headed

I later asked Jimmy, "Are such dire events contemplated by the prophets? Where does God say history is headed?"

Jimmy replied, "We talked about the fact that the nations that are going to align themselves will basically be the Middle Eastern Islamic Arab nations, with one exception—Russia, which is the Magog of Ezekiel 38:2. But not too long down the road—by 2010 to 2012—we are going to see the demographics in Russia change and Muslims will comprise the majority of the people not only in the populace but in the military as well. But Iran is a major player in all that happens, and today it is the number one enemy of Israel. Israel and the world, in fact, are focused on what's happening in Iran. That is not happenstance; that is Bible prophecy preparing for its ultimate fulfillment."

During the days we were taping our documentary series in Israel, some of our Israeli guides asked, "Why are you presenting this information to your television audience?"

I responded, "The reason we are sharing this material is so that people will come to understand the Bible's prophecies and realize that Jesus Christ is the Son of God. He is the coming Messiah, and He is coming back. I think that when people hear about prophecy, they think of scatterbrained ideas by people who don't know what they are talking about. But what we're putting before them is solid evidence that anybody can see—gigantic evidence that should preach a message all by itself to them if they would just look."

Jimmy added, "If you know Jesus Christ as Lord and Savior, you must be a student of Bible prophecy. One in every three pages in the Bible is prophetic. God has a plan, and we are seeing that plan unfold on a daily basis. You cannot read the newspaper and you cannot listen to the television news reports without seeing God at work in our world today."

To those traveling with us, Jimmy shared, "In light of the fact that current events are so connected with Bible prophecy, you need to make sure you are prepared for Jesus Christ to come back at any moment. And then, once you know Christ, commit yourself to pure living. Paul told Titus that God's grace 'teaches us to say "No" to ungodliness and worldly passions, and to live self-controlled, upright and godly lives in this present age, while we wait for the blessed hope—the glorious appearing of our great God and Savior, Jesus Christ' (Titus 2:12-13). And as you look for Him, be productive until He does come. He could in fact come today."

It is the belief that Christ is returning soon that leads us into the third part of our book, in which we discuss plans for the future Jewish temple and explain the teachings of the book of Revelation. Many people think the book of Revelation is confusing rather than help-ful; as a result, they neglect the study of Revelation. That's why in the fourth part of this book, we will take a five-part walk through the book of Revelation. As we do, we believe you'll be encouraged and inspired as you begin to more deeply understand God's ultimate plan for the end times.

PART THREE

# PREPARATIONS FOR THE FUTURE JEWISH TEMPLE

## Chapter 9

# PREPARATIONS FOR THE TEMPLE: THE PLANS AND PEOPLE

Years ago, I (Jimmy) sat in my office in New York City with one of the most controversial Jewish rabbis in the world sitting across from me. I was about to learn that there was a movement among certain Jews to do things that, if successful, would answer the prayers of thousands of Jewish people from the last 2,000 years. That Jewish rabbi was a charismatic individual—Rabbi Meir Kahana—and the prayers he would answer were in regard to the rebuilding of a Jewish temple on the Temple Mount in Jerusalem.

I first met Meir Kahana when he was introduced to me at a radio station where I had once worked. The rabbi was meeting with me to discuss the possibility of starting his own weekly radio show. It was during this time that I shared my personal story about my faith in Jesus Christ. I shared with Meir Kahana, an Orthodox Jew, the plan of salvation for not only Jewish people but also for the whole world. The rabbi listened very attentively, then responded with a startling statement. He expressed the belief that I was "there for such a time as this," and that everything either one of us did must be for the "glory of God" because what God does is for "His holy namesake."

I also learned that the rabbi had one driving desire: to build the

Third Temple in Jerusalem. I immediately asked him *why* he wanted to rebuild the temple. He said: "I know that the day the Third Temple is completed, the Messiah will come."

## Why a Third Temple?

The rabbi's mention of the Third Temple marked the first time I began to realize that many Jewish people were working toward making the Third Temple a reality. Even today, three times daily, there are prayers offered up by Jews who gather at the Western Wall in Jerusalem, crying out, "May our temple be rebuilt in this day here in the holy city."

Over the years, my investigation into the personalities and the projects involved in the preparations for the temple have brought me into contact with an interesting cast of people and organizations. In fact, the rabbi's own brother, Nachman Kahana, would come into focus as the philosophical leader of this modern-day temple movement.

This interest in rebuilding the temple has been a part of the Jewish fabric down through the centuries since Herod's Temple (the Second Temple) was destroyed by General Titus and his Roman Army in A.D. 70. As already mentioned, the Jewish people pray daily for the rebuilding of the temple to begin immediately.

In the course of my research, I was encouraged to meet one man, a former member of the Jerusalem city council, who had started an organization to get the attention of the Jewish world for the purpose of rebuilding the temple.

## The Temple Mount Faithful

The name of that man is Gershon Salomon, a person who had the unique opportunity of being shown around the Temple Mount only a few days after the Jewish people had reunited the City of Jerusalem during the Six-Day War in 1967. It was not long after that Gershon started a movement called the Temple Mount Faithful. This group formed an organization to encourage the Jewish world to follow the biblical mandate to once again establish God's house in Jerusalem.

The Jordanian guide who originally showed Gershon Salomon around the Temple Mount in June 1967 told Gershon that he believed the Jewish people had come to Jerusalem to rebuild their temple. This guide even told Gershon that Muslims believe the Jews will one day restore their worship in Jerusalem by rebuilding their temple on the Temple Mount.

Gershon Salomon and the Temple Mount Faithful might have started the process to rebuild the temple in 1967 if the Israeli government had not given control of the Temple Mount to the Jordanians under an arrangement designed to appease the Arab world. Today the Temple Mount is monitored by an Islamic trust called the Waqf, yet there is a big struggle that continues today between the Palestinians and the Jordanians as to who has the authority to provide care for the Temple Mount, even though the Israeli government legally owns all of the property.

## Control of the Temple Court

The control of the Temple Mount and the preparation to build a temple on the spot now occupied by the Muslim Dome of the Rock has become a point of great concern in the Arab world. A Jewish temple on the Temple Mount would jeopardize the Muslim Palestinian ambition to name Jerusalem as their state capital.

In fact, in the summer of 1998, the Conference of Islamic Foreign Ministers met in Casablanca under the presidency of Morocco's King Hassan II. The conference was called to discuss the question of Jerusalem and was viewed as an integral part of an offensive against Israel.

At this meeting, the Palestinian leader Yasser Arafat told the Islamic foreign ministers that "Israel has already announced its desire to start a war over the Holy City of Jerusalem, and has declared its plans regarding the Holy Temple." Arafat stated, "Israel's sole goal since its conquest of Jerusalem in 1967 has been to 'purify' and 'Judaize' Jerusalem." Arafat added, "Of late, Israel has initiated the great war to make Jerusalem 'Israeli' in order to kill our master, Mohammed."

The ancient Jewish prophets predicted there will be a major conflict over Jerusalem in the last days. The Bible also predicts there will one day be a third Jewish temple at the same location as the two previous temples. This mandate has motivated a segment of Orthodox Judaism to actively prepare for the construction of this coming temple.

## The Temple Institute

Right now, there is another Jewish group in Jerusalem making preparations for the Third Temple—the Temple Institute. The Temple Institute is a collective of scholars headed up by Rabbi Israel Ariel. These leaders have studied the Old Testament requirements for preparing the priest, the priestly garments, the musical instruments, and the implements for the sacrifices and worship at the temple. These rabbis have already commissioned artisans to make the items needed to operate the Third Temple.

For the first time in almost 2,000 years there are people preparing to carry out services at a future temple in Jerusalem. The personalities involved in the preparations are fervently dedicated to the cause.

For students of Bible prophecy, this Temple Mount movement evidences one of the most outstanding signs of the soon coming of the Messiah. Though there has been a desire to build another temple in Jerusalem over the last 2,000 years, there has never been so much progress toward making it happen. For many, this is strong evidence that the Lord's return truly is near.

## Priestly Preparations

When I (Jimmy) met with Rabbi Nachman Kahana in his yeshiva in Jerusalem—a place of learning for young Jewish men—he was working at his computer. He told me he was using the computer to study the Torah, the first five books of the Old Testament. He also mentioned a special database he kept on his computer. Kahana shared that this database contained the names of all the Jewish men in the world who were qualified to become priests. When I asked why he had collected this information, he answered, "Because we have contacted them to come here to Jerusalem to prepare to be the priests who will operate the temple when it stands in Jerusalem."

"Why do you need these men to come here to Jerusalem to study the priestly duties?" I asked Kahana.

"Because we are going to build a temple here in the holy city, and we need priests to operate it."

## Studying for the Priesthood

How does a prospective Jewish priest prepare to serve in the future Jewish temple? The Old Testament book of Leviticus was written largely as a textbook for priestly candidates. The first seven chapters of Leviticus teach us about the temple sacrifices. Chapters 8-10 provide the standards for a person who would serve as a Jewish priest. And the final 17 chapters detail the system of worship for the temple complex.

Traditionally, Jewish boys would begin their study of Leviticus at the age of two. The boy's mother would start reading the book to him from the time he was first learning to speak. Since a man qualified to serve as a Jewish priest cannot do so until he is 30 years old, those taught according to this tradition will study Leviticus for 28 years before becoming a priest.

I asked Rabbi Kahana, "How could anyone know whether he is qualified to be a priest? After all, the genealogical records were destroyed in A.D. 70. Wouldn't it be impossible to know which Jewish men are qualified to serve as priests in the next temple?"

Kahana said this information was handed down by word of mouth.

The father would pass the tradition on to his son, from one generation to another, so that those who were qualified would be aware of their status. He also joked that no one would be foolish enough to claim to be a member of the priestly family if he was not truly qualified. "They have many restrictions on them, including the way they live, who they marry, how they eat, what they wear, and many other requirements laid out in their priestly manuals."

In 1 Chronicles 23:4, the Bible reveals that there were to be 24,000 priests set aside to "supervise the work of the temple of the LORD" (1 Chronicles 23:4). I asked the rabbi if there were that many men in Jerusalem studying to become priests. Rabbi Kahana did not reveal any specific numbers about how many priests were in training, but he seemed to indicate there were enough men in training to fulfill the biblical requirements.

## The Priestly Garments

In addition to carrying out their duties, priests of the Jewish temple were required to wear very specific clothing. When I asked Rabbi Kahana about these garments, he said that many of these garments had already been made and were in storage in preparation for the future temple.

The garments worn by the priests were to be dignified and beautiful, as precious as the garments of royalty, according to the instructions God gave to Moses. The Bible attaches much significance to the garments, including specific requirements. For example, each garment must not be sewn, but instead woven in a special manner, out of one piece of cloth, without seams. The arms are woven separately, and these can be attached by sewing them to the rest of the garment.

The Bible mentions three categories of priestly garments. First is the high priest's apparel that was worn year round, which consisted of eight garments called *the golden garments*. Second, there were four *white garments* worn by the high priest on the Day of Atonement. Third, there were the four *uniforms of the ordinary priests.* These four garments, worn all year long by the ordinary priests, were identical to the white garments worn by the high priest on the Day of Atonement.

The priestly clothing also included an item called an *ephod.* An ephod was similar in shape to an apron and was worn on the top of the other garments of the high priest. The breastplate was fastened to the ephod, and gold chains were attached to the two square settings fixed on the shoulders of the high priest. The breastplate was square-shaped and worn over the heart of the high priest.

The breastplate was called the *breastplate of judgment* or *decision* because of the unique role it played in helping to render fateful decisions for the Jewish people. Those decisions were revealed through the stones attached to the breastplate. There were twelve stones on the breastplate—four rows of three stones each—with each stone representing one of the twelve tribes of Israel. Each stone was engraved with the name of one of the tribes.

Each priest, including the high priest, was also required to wear a headdress. The high priest would wear a turban on his head in such a way as to allow for the crown to be worn as part of his attire. Many researchers believe that the ordinary priests' hats were exactly the same as that of the high priest, except the ordinary priests had their hats wound on them, and the high priest simply had his turban placed on his head.

The priests' garment had a sash, made of white linen, which went around the priests' waist. This belt was wrapped many times around the body. Its purpose was to separate the upper body from the lower body, and it was required by Jewish law during prayer or the mention of anything holy.

The priests wore no shoes or sandals in their service to the temple. They walked barefoot on the marble floors of the temple courts. They did so to preserve the sanctity of not only the temple itself, but also the entire temple complex.

According to those involved in the Temple Institute, many—if not all—of these garments have already been made and are now in storage in Jerusalem. Each one has been designed with the utmost care.

But the priests and their garments aren't the only things in place. In our next chapter, we'll learn about some of the other tools created in recent years for use in the future Jewish temple. And we'll find out more about the location of the lost Ark of the Covenant.

# Chapter 10:

# PREPARATIONS FOR THE TEMPLE: THE TOOLS AND THE MODERN SANHEDRIN

There is much activity taking place today among Jews who are preparing for the rebuilding of the temple on the Temple Mount in Jerusalem. Twenty-four thousand priests, the training of these priests, and a myriad of garments to suit these leaders make up a massive undertaking. And there is far more being done in anticipation of the future temple's operation.

Rabbi Kahana revealed that the implements necessary to start operation of the temple have already been created. The Temple Institute (mentioned in the last chapter), comprised of dedicated Orthodox Jews who are on the cutting edge in all the preparations for the next temple, have these implements in storage. This institute, located in Jerusalem, can even be visited. And some of the implements are on display.

The Temple Institute is made up of a combination of biblical scholars and artisans. The scholars research the items needed to operate the temple and the artisans are then commissioned to build the implements. From what we have observed, their work has been meticulous.

Some of the implements already prepared for temple service include the crown for the high priest, the menorah, the table for the showbread, the altar of incense, the *mizraq,* the lots for the scapegoat, and instruments to be used by the priests. The Temple Institute has these items available so the priestly candidates can acquaint themselves with them.

## Temple Tools

During one of my (Jimmy) many visits to the institute, a Jewish man who intends to be one of the priests at the coming temple was on duty, and he explained to me the requirements for the implements and the form of service for each of these items.

### The High Priestly Crown

The crown for the high priest is made out of 24-karat gold. It is designed to adjust to fit the head of the one designated by the Jewish Sanhedrin as the high priest. This is made possible by attaching a blue cord to the open-ended crown. The reason 24-karat gold is used is so that the crown is pliable enough to conform to the headdress of the high priest.

### The Menorah

Some have suggested that the original menorah from the first Jewish temple is in the basement of the Vatican in Rome. There is a story that General Titus and the Roman army carried it back to Rome after destroying the Second Temple in A.D. 70. In Rome, a relief on the Arch of Titus indicates the menorah was included in the temple treasures captured by the Romans when they sacked Jerusalem.

Because of that possibility, the Israeli government dispatched the minister of religious affairs to Rome in 1996 to ask the pope to either confirm or deny the Vatican's possession of the menorah. The pope would neither confirm nor deny, but he did hint that he may return the menorah to Israel someday.

The Temple Institute, choosing not to rely on the possibility that the original menorah is in the Vatican's possession, has designed its own menorah for use in the next temple. The artisans at the institute built this full-sized menorah based on a model they had on display for many years. A replica of the original, it is a gold-plated candle stand consisting of 90 pounds of gold. This menorah is currently on display under tight security, overlooking the Western Wall Plaza in the Old City of Jerusalem.

### The Table of Showbread

The unique shape of the table of showbread has been the subject of much study at the Temple Institute. The preparation of the bread placed on the table has been a mystery for the scholars to unfold as well. After much research, the institute has been able to construct the table of showbread, and they also claim to have the special formula for preparing the bread. So they can now make 12 loaves that are to be placed on the table of showbread. These items, then, are ready for the temple.

### The Mizraq

A *mizraq* is simply a water pitcher. Many *mizraqot* are needed for the priests to carry out the daily sacrifices, and to conduct the Jewish festivals. Some of the *mizraq* can be made of pure silver and some of pure gold.

The *mizraq* does not have a base; that is because the *mizraq* cannot be set down by the priests during their administration of sacrificial duties. Should they set down the *mizraq*—which contains the blood of goats, lambs, or bulls—the blood could clot and become contaminated.

During the Feast of Passover there will be a need for a great number of *mizraqot* to be available to the priests to fulfill the Levitical requirements for the Passover sacrifice. The magnitude of the Passover feast requires that a large number of priests participate, and that they use hundreds of these *mizraqot*. The institute has a number of *mizraqot* and continues to produce more.

### Additional Tools

There are many other implements necessary for the operation of the next temple. The silver cup and the golden flask, created by the researchers and craftsmen at the institute, must be used in the ceremony of the water libation. The incense chalice, which holds the ingredients for the incense offering, is available for service, along with the different kinds of incense to be used.

The very first service performed by the priests in the First and Second Temples every day—at the first rays of dawn—was the removal of the ashes left upon the altar. A silver shovel, always kept at the southwest corner of the altar, is now on hand for this task. Another vessel— needed for use by the high priest on the Day of Atonement—is the lottery box, which contains the lots that are to be cast to determine which of the goats would be designated the scapegoat.

Before the priests can tend to the offerings on the altar, they must sanctify their hands and feet with water from a copper washbasin. A reconstructed washbasin is at the Temple Institute awaiting service at the temple. The silver trumpets, fashioned after information gleaned from Talmudic sources and the artwork on the relief on the Arch of Titus, are on display and stand ready for a priest to sound forth during the sacrificial service.

All of the aforementioned implements are prepared, stored, and awaiting the building of the temple. In fact, there are enough implements available to start operation of the temple today.

## The Harps

One requirement of a fully functioning Jewish temple is the availability of a large Levitical orchestra to play music for the worship services. Among the instruments needed for this orchestra are many Jewish harps.

The answer to this dilemma came from a home on King David Street in Jerusalem. The home was that of Micah and Shoshanna Harrari. Micah had been a finish carpenter, and for fun, he once built his own handcrafted guitar.

One day, Shoshanna asked Micah to make her a harp for her upcoming birthday. Micah's first response was that he did not know how to build a harp. Yet Micah wanted to surprise his wife for her birthday, so he made his way to the Jezreel Valley in the center part of the State of Israel, where he found a picture of a ten-string harp that was carved on the wall of a cave near Megiddo.

Micah copied the image and returned back to Jerusalem to begin work on the harp. When the harp was completed, Micah and Shoshanna were contacted by *The Jerusalem Post* for a feature story in the newspaper.

The couple later discovered that the harp Micah had built was the first harp made in almost 2,000 years in Israel. The need for harps had diminished with the destruction of Herod's temple in A.D. 70. During the temple era, the high priest had complied with King David's request for a large orchestra to play for the worship activities (1 Chronicles 23:5). This large orchestra included cymbals, psalteries, trumpets, and harps. It has been determined that a large number of the 4,000 Levites who served the temple orchestra played harps. For the Third Temple, then, someone was needed who could produce harps. Now, for the first time in 2,000 years in Israel, someone was making biblical harps. In fact, the Temple Institute commissioned Micah to produce all of the harps needed for the Levite orchestra that will perform when the temple is in full operation.

Shortly after the story about the ten-string harp ran in *The Jerusalem Post,* an elderly rabbi showed up at the House of Harrari and wanted to know if they really did have such a harp. When Shoshanna showed the old rabbi the harp, he asked if he could hold it. Standing there clutching the harp, the rabbi began to cry. Shoshanna quickly asked the rabbi if everything was all right, to which he answered yes.

The rabbi then explained why he had become emotional. He said that the ancient Jewish Talmud recorded an old Jewish tradition that when a ten-string harp shows up in Jerusalem, that would be the time of the coming of the Messiah.

## The Lost Ark

Is the lost Ark of the Covenant really lost? Some say the Ark is not lost after all. Some sources indicate the Ark can be found exactly where it was placed over 2,500 years ago. Even though there has been much talk, study, and intrigue about the whereabouts of the Ark, its location is still unknown. The Ark, which was the center of Jewish worship for 2,000 years, is an essential part of the future temple.

Much has been written about the Ark being in Ethiopia. That rumor says that when the Queen of Sheba visited King Solomon around 1000 B.C, Solomon was so infatuated with the queen that he gave her the Ark to take back home. The story then says that the Ark went to Ethiopia almost 3,000 years ago, and has been handed down through the royal families to the present day.

There have even been reports that some Ethiopians who immigrated to Israel in 1991 during Operation Solomon secretly brought the Ark with them to Israel. Yet those reports have been found baseless.

The Ark has most likely never left the land of Israel since the time it was brought into the Promised Land at the time of Joshua's conquest. Both the Bible and extrabiblical Jewish writings state that the Ark is hidden in a location the Levites had prepared for times of war or danger. In 2 Chronicles 35 we read details about the times prior to the dispersion of the Jewish people during the Babylonian captivity. The ruler of Judah, King Josiah, believed the temple would come under attack by the Babylonians. He instructed the Levites to take the Ark and "put [it] in the house" (2 Chronicles 35:3). He was not referring to the temple when he used the word "house," but the place that King Solomon had previously prepared to keep the Ark safe. We can know this because the Ark had already been in the "house" (or temple) for almost 400 years by this time. King Solomon had built the temple and had placed the Ark in the "Holy of Holies" around 1000 B.C. (1 Kings 8:1-11).

Also, the word used for "house" in Hebrew is *bayit*, which means "a special place, a shelter, in the inward parts." It refers to a location that was under the Holy of Holies, which today is underneath the Dome of the Rock on the Temple Mount. The Talmud states that the Ark can be found there. It is that statement in the Talmud that led two rabbis to search for the lost Ark in 1982.

The first rabbi was Shlomo Goren. He was the chief rabbi of the Israeli Defense Force in 1967. On June 7, when Israel took back the Old City of Jerusalem, including the Western Wall, Rabbi Goren offered the first Jewish prayer at the reclaimed Western Wall in hundreds of years. He was also the first rabbi to blow a *shofar* (Jewish trumpet— usually made from a ram's horn) at the wall.

The second rabbi, Rabbi Yehuda Getz, was the chief rabbi of the Jewish holy sites in Israel. That responsibility included the Western Wall, an extremely holy site to the Jewish people. Rabbi Getz was so important that the Orthodox Jewish leader gave him oversight of the synagogue closest to the location of the original Holy of Holies.

In 1982 these two rabbis decided to go under the Temple Mount to see if the Ark was still there. They broke through the Western Wall at what is called the Warren Gate. Continuing underground, they claim to have seen—but not reached—the Ark of the Covenant. Rabbi Getz told of the sighting of the ark in an interview for my (Jimmy's) documentary on the Third Temple, *Ready to Rebuild*.

I (Jimmy) personally had the opportunity to interview Rabbi Goren about his experience with the Ark. He shared that he had come within 25 feet of touching the most important piece of temple furniture. When I asked Goren why he did not bring the Ark out from beneath the

Temple Mount, he replied, "We will bring the Ark out from its hiding place when there is a place [a temple] to put the Ark."

Both of these rabbis, Yehuda Getz and Shlomo Goren, are now dead, but they have passed along information about their findings to associates who claim to know the exact whereabouts of the Ark. These associates plan to reveal the Ark at the appropriate time when the Jewish temple is rebuilt.

## The Sanhedrin

It was during my interview with Rabbi Goren that I first learned about the plans for the modern reforming of the Sanhedrin. This group of 70 male Jewish leaders is required for the operation of the future temple, because only the Sanhedrin can select the man who will serve as the high priest of the temple.

The word *Sanhedrin* comes from the Greek word *synedrion,* meaning "a council" or "meeting place." In the Bible, the Sanhedrin was the governing body or supreme council of the Jews and functioned as both a religious and civil court. The people of ancient Israel would stand before the Temple Mount to have their questions answered or their causes heard and decided by the smaller Sanhedrin of 23 or by the greater Sanhedrin.

The power of the Sanhedrin would, of course, vary with political circumstances. Sometimes it was almost absolute, while at other times it was limited to religious authority. The Sanhedrin was in full force, however, at the time of Jesus. It was an institution that exerted decisive influence on the future of Israel. The members made legal determinations that the traditionalists declared absolutely binding on all, and of greater obligation than Scripture itself.

The Sanhedrin can be traced back to 70 men who were appointed by Moses to assist him in his duties. In the time of Jesus, it was comprised of 71 members: 70 elders and scribes, plus the high priest. This group usually met near the temple in Jerusalem. The Sanhedrin could issue judicial sentences, but only the Roman procurator could ratify and carry out a death sentence. The Great Sanhedrin in Israel exercised supreme spiritual authority and in that capacity settled all religious questions. The Sanhedrin was finally dismantled when Jerusalem was destroyed in A.D. 70.

One of the obligations of the Sanhedrin was that they meet within the confines of the temple complex. It is a fact that the meeting room that has been prepared by Rabbi Goren's people is not currently located within the boundaries of the ancient temples, or even on the Temple Mount. But that is not a problem because Ezekiel prophesied that the next temple complex will cover an area of one square mile (Ezekiel 42:20).

The present size of the Temple Mount is approximately three football fields. The size of the entire Old City of Jerusalem today, including the Jewish, Christian, Muslim, and Armenian Quarters, is about one square mile—the exact size of the coming temple complex called for by the Old Testament prophets. The people preparing to build the next temple want to follow the Scriptures as closely as possible. Therefore, the room Goren's people have prepared for the Sanhedrin will be located within the boundaries of the future temple complex.

When I (Jimmy) was talking with Professor Hillel Wise a couple of years ago, I asked him about the selection of the high priest. As a spokesperson for the newly formed Sanhedrin, he said a high priest would have to be elected. Then he said *they already have in mind the person who will serve as high priest.* I have had opportunity to be in this man's home. He is a brilliant man with multiple doctoral degrees, and he is an expert in both the Jewish Scriptures and the Talmud.

Those involved in the plans for the rebuilding of the Jewish temple have taken on this task with extreme seriousness. They have plans in place to begin worship on the Temple Mount as soon as they are given access to it.

# PART FOUR

# INVESTIGATING ISRAEL IN THE BOOK OF REVELATION

# Chapter 11

# THE THREE PILLARS OF THE BOOK OF REVELATION

Today, one out of every four Christian adults believes Jesus could return in their lifetime. And the book of Revelation is God's message to all of us who want to understand what is to come. It contains Jesus Christ's last words to the church on such important doctrines as the rapture, the second coming, and the final judgment. It reveals what will ultimately happen to Satan, the Antichrist, and those who follow false religions. Jesus warns of the terrible future events that will take place on earth during the Tribulation, the battle of Armageddon, and His second coming to earth. In this book, He tells about the millennium, the final judgment of every person who has ever lived, and what God has planned for His people in eternity future.

In the following chapters, we will take you step by step through the book of Revelation in a clear and concise manner so that you can understand its message, especially as it relates to the nation of Israel.

As we begin, please don't be intimidated. We know a lot of people who have said, "I can never understand the book of Revelation." But God has given us the book of Revelation for a reason. He wants us to know about the end times, which is relevant to all that is happening in Israel today.

## Why Is Revelation So Important?

Why do we believe understanding Revelation is so important? First, the Bible says in 2 Timothy 3:16, "All Scripture is God-breathed, and is useful." God uses the Bible to prepare and equip His people to do every good work (see verse 17). All 66 books of the Bible are worth studying.

Second, in Revelation 1:3 we read, "Blessed is the one who reads the words of this prophecy, and blessed are those who hear it and take to heart what is written in it, because the time is near." So we have a guaranteed blessing if we study the book of Revelation. Third, in Revelation 19:10, we read that "the testimony of Jesus is the spirit of prophecy." This book, which reveals Jesus Christ, lifts up our wonderful Savior, and it is important that we study it.

That's the biblical perspective, but there's a political perspective to this as well. As we look at the latest developments in our world today, we can go to the book of Revelation and better understand what we see unfolding around us.

Let's begin by learning about Revelation's title, author, setting, and time of writing.

## The Title

The first verse in this book, Revelation 1:1, says, "This is a revelation of Jesus Christ." Very simply, this book reveals Jesus Christ in His person, His power, and His program. This book comes from God the Father and was given to Jesus, who then delegated an angel to give the message of Revelation to John the Revelator.

## The Author, Setting, and Time

John was the pastor at the church at Ephesus, a city in Asia Minor, in what is now known as Turkey. Ephesus was on the coast of the Aegean Sea. About A.D. 95, Domitian, who was the Roman emperor at the time, told John that because of his testimony for Jesus Christ—because he proclaimed and upheld the Word of God so strongly—he was going to be sent to an island in the middle of the Aegean Sea, the Isle of Patmos. Patmos is only three miles wide and six miles long. Yet there are 365 churches today on the Isle of Patmos!

In the opening of Revelation we read that John was to write down seven messages for seven different churches. Not only was John a pastor at the church at Ephesus, he also had connections with the other six churches mentioned in chapters 2 and 3 of Revelation. We're not sure whether he had started those churches or he was an overseer of those churches. Regardless, he had some kind of relationship with each one, and he would pass along the message intended for each one.

## Interpreting Revelation

Historically, there have been four ways to interpret the book of Revelation. Before moving ahead, we'll take a moment to look at these four ways of interpretation, then we'll explain which one we hold to in this book.

The first method of interpretation is the *allegorical approach,* or a nonliteral interpretation of Revelation. The allegorical approach came into practice many years ago because people studying the Word of God were able to literally accept verses such as John 3:16 (God so loved the world that He gave His one and only Son), but they could not understand, for example, the book of Daniel, Ezekiel, or Revelation in particular. Thus they would turn to the allegorical approach. This approach views Revelation as somewhat of a fairy tale or a nice little story about how good and evil will play out in the end times.

Bible interpreter Roy Zuck makes these observations about an allegorical approach to Scripture:

> Allegorizing is searching for a hidden or a secret meaning underlying but remote from and unrelated in reality to the

more obvious meaning of a text…In this approach the literal is superficial; the allegorical is the true meaning.[10]

In other words, an allegorical approach leads toward a personal interpretation that lacks external evidence to justify it. As a result, those who interpret Revelation allegorically rarely agree on the interpretations they come up with.

Second, there is the *preterist approach.* This approach applies the allegorical method of interpretation, but then says the book of Revelation had to be written by A.D. 65 and was completely fulfilled in A.D. 70. Why? A.D. 70 was the year that Titus led the Roman army into Jerusalem. The Romans devastated the city, destroyed the temple, and dispersed the Jewish people to the four corners of the earth. The preterist approach to interpreting Revelation starts with the assumption that everything in the book was fulfilled in A.D. 70. Therefore, Revelation does not apply to future events. However, this approach to Revelation fails because the historical evidence from 20 early church fathers tells us the book was written in A.D. 95.

Dr. Mark Hitchcock, one of today's top experts on the date of the book of Revelation in relation to the interpretation of Bible prophecy, has shared the historical difficulty with the preterist position: "Writing in A.D. 170, [the church father] Irenaeus, who grew up in Smyrna, who knew Polycarp who knew the apostle John [Polycarp was a direct disciple of the apostle John who wrote Revelation], says that the apocalyptic vision was seen towards the end of Domitian's reign, and Domitian's reign ended in A.D. 96."[11]

Third, there is the *historical approach* to interpreting Revelation. This method takes the entire book of Revelation and applies it to periods of time throughout the church age, or the last 2,000 years. In other words, Revelation is said to describe the various eras in church history. However, those who follow this approach do not agree on which events in past history apply to which passages of Scripture in Revelation.

Fourth, there is what is called *the futuristic* or *literal approach* to interpreting the book of Revelation. This is the approach taken in this book. We believe that the first three chapters of Revelation are past and present. But from Revelation 4:2 to the end, everything that is described has not yet happened. These prophecies will literally be fulfilled after a special event known as the rapture of the church.

## Understanding Apocalyptic Literature

Using the futuristic or literal approach, we find that God has given us a timeline for the Jewish people, the Gentiles, and Christians. He put them in three different books of the Bible. We will talk about that shortly, but let's answer these questions:

1. What is apocalyptic literature?
2. Why did Jesus deliver His message using apocalyptic terms?

During the early generations of human history, from creation until the time of Abraham in Genesis 12, the earth was inhabited solely by Gentiles (non-Jews). From Genesis 12 to Acts 1, human history is populated by both Gentiles and Jews. Then from Acts 2, the Day of Pentecost, when the church was brought into existence, on into eternity future, through chapter 22 of the book of Revelation, you have all three members of the human family—Gentiles, Jews, and Christians.

Three different books of the Bible detail the history of each group. First, the book of Daniel is a timeline for *Gentiles*. It starts at the time of the Babylonian captivity and takes Gentiles into eternity future. Second, the book of *Ezekiel* is a timeline for Jews. It also starts at the Babylonian captivity, and takes Jews into eternity future. Third, the book of *Revelation* starts with the resurrection of Jesus Christ, mentioned in Revelation 1:18, and then helps Christians understand what is going to happen in the future after the rapture of the church.

The basic principle behind apocalyptic literature is that it will use symbols. Now, the use of symbols does not mean we are talking about a fairy tale, fable, or allegory. Rather, a symbol can communicate an absolute truth. For example, Revelation 1 talks about Jesus standing among seven golden candlesticks (verses 12-13). Then we read that He has seven stars in His hand (verse 16). That's apocalyptic language: the seven candlesticks are the seven churches of Asia Minor, and the seven stars are the angels of the seven churches (verse 20). Apocalyptic literature will interpret itself and convey absolute truths.

## The Big Picture of Revelation

It is vital to realize that the best way to understand the book of Revelation is to study it chronologically. To understand the big picture, the verses in Revelation must be looked at and understood within a chronological unfolding of the events that corresponds with other biblical passages.

### THE THREE PILLARS OF REVELATION

| PILLAR 1 | PILLAR 2 | PILLAR 3 |
|---|---|---|
| Rev. 4:1 | Rev. 19:10–20:10 | Rev. 20:11-15 |
| *The Rapture* | *The Return* | *The Retribution* |
| This instant "taking up" of Christians from earth into the presence of Jesus Christ begins the seven-year Tribulation, consisting of 21 judgments. | Christ returns as King and leads His 1000-year millennial kingdom that ends with a defeat of Satan, the false prophet, and the Antichrist. | The Great White Throne Judgment takes place and is followed by a new Jerusalem, a new heaven, and a new earth for eternity future. |

## The Three Pillars

To begin, imagine that you have three pillars. These three pillars represent the three main events in the future as recorded for us in the book of Revelation. The *first pillar,* from left to right, represents the next event on the prophetic calendar, which is the rapture of the church. Jesus will shout, the trumpet of God will sound, the archangel will shout, and then those of us who know Christ as Lord and Savior will be caught up into the heavenlies. We believe that chronologically, Revelation chapter 4 marks the rapture of the church, an event described in 1 Thessalonians 4:16-18 (NASB):

> For the Lord Himself will descend from heaven with a shout, with the voice of an archangel and with the trumpet of God, and the dead in Christ will rise first. Then we who are alive *and* remain shall be caught up together with them in the clouds to meet the Lord in the air. And thus we shall always be with the Lord. Therefore comfort one another with these words.

The word *rapture* comes from the Latin Vulgate translation of the Bible, which renders the word translated "caught up" as *raptus,* which literally means "to carry off" or "to seize." The original Greek word here is *harpazo,* which means "to snatch out" or "to seize."

Jesus told the church at Philadelphia, "Since you have kept My command to endure patiently, I will keep you from the hour of trial that is going to come upon the whole world." This hour of trial, the Tribulation, which is going to come upon the whole world, is something Jesus promises to keep Christians *from.* Notice Jesus does not promise to keep Christians "through" the time of the Tribulation, but "from" the entire time period, the hour of trial, all seven years of the Tribulation, which is described in Revelation 6–19. How will He do that? Through the rapture, when He will catch up into the air all who have trusted Him as their Savior.

Paul told the Thessalonian church, "You turned to God from idols to serve the living and true God, and to wait for his Son from heaven, whom he raised from the dead—Jesus, who delivers us from the coming wrath" (1 Thessalonians 1:10). How will Jesus deliver Christians from the wrath of the Tribulation? By taking them up into the air at the rapture.

Revelation 4:1 occurs before the Tribulation, which is depicted in chapters 6 through 19. Therefore, we believe Revelation 4:1 is when the rapture takes place. In a moment, we will present other reasons we believe the Bible teaches the rapture occurs before the Tribulation.

In Revelation 4:1, John wrote, "After these things I looked and behold, a door standing open in heaven, and the first voice which I had heard, like the sound of a trumpet speaking with me, said, 'Come up here, and I will show you what must take place after these things.' Immediately I was in the Spirit; and behold, a throne was standing in heaven, and One sitting on the throne."

Because John's experiences are similar to what will happen at the rapture when the church is caught up to heaven, some have equated the two events. But John was not raptured, and his natural body was probably still on the Isle of Patmos. Accordingly, it is better to regard this as a special situation. But from the context in which this event is placed in the book of Revelation, it is reasonable to conclude that the rapture has taken place. What John is seeing is a setting of the stage for the events that will take place in heaven and on earth in the period after the rapture.[12] The things he saw from chapters 6 through 19 all take place during the Tribulation, the terrible "hour of trial of trial that is going to come upon the whole world."

Moving on, we find the *second pillar* in Revelation 19:11, which describes the second coming of Christ back to the earth. He is riding on a white horse, and we who are in the heavenlies with Him—having gone there at the rapture of the church—will come back on white horses as well. That will be followed by a 1,000-year period of time called the millennium; which is described in Revelation 20:1-6. The *third pillar* (or major event) is the final judgment of the world. Described in Revelation 20:11-15, this even is called the Great White Throne Judgment.

These three pillars form the basis of our road map through the book of Revelation. And around these three pillars we can place every single verse in Revelation and place it in the era of history during which it will take place.

## Beginning Our Journey Through Revelation

Throughout the remainder of this chapter, we'll provide a quick overview of the contents of Revelation as a whole. Then, in the following chapters, we'll go back and explain further details regarding additional aspects of Revelation that fit within this framework.

Prior to the first pillar—the rapture of the church—Revelation 1 presents the person and power of Jesus Christ. Next, chapters 2 and 3 report the last words of Jesus Christ to the church. If you desire personal revival, chapters 2 and 3 of Revelation are the place to begin. Those seven letters to the body of Christ today are profound and powerful, offering encouragement and challenges to seven churches that existed in Asia Minor when the apostle John wrote the book.

As we have mentioned, the rapture of the church takes place at Revelation 4:1. Jesus and the archangel will shout and the trumpet of God will sound and Christians will be caught up to be with Jesus in the air. In Revelation 5:5-12, we see a great choir of angels singing, "Worthy is the lamb." Then chapter 6 begins the first of three sets of seven judgments: seven seal judgments, seven trumpet judgments, and seven vial or bowl judgments.

This seven-year period of time called the Tribulation has two parts. During the first three-and-a-half years there are seven seal judgments. Further, there will be two witnesses who will preach and 144,000 male virgin Jews (Revelation 7:4-8; 14:1-5) who will come to know Jesus Christ as Lord and Savior. During this time they will travel around the world preaching the gospel of the kingdom (Matthew 24:14).

According to Revelation 11:3-12, at the end of the three-and-a-half years, the two witnesses who preach the gospel will be killed and will lie in the streets of Jerusalem for three-and-a-half days. The entire world will witness that event. These two men will then be resurrected and ascend into the heavenlies. At the midway point of the Tribulation period, there will be a fight in the heavenlies between the good angels, led by Michael the archangel, and Satan and all of his evil angels (Revelation

20:7-9). Satan's angels will be cast upon the earth and start to attack the nation of Israel. This time marks another future connection to Israel being under fire.

The Bible then says that in the last three-and-a-half years of the Tribulation period there will come seven trumpet judgments and seven vial judgments. These judgments will culminate with kings out of the east coming to join the Antichrist to fight the Battle of Armageddon. And when this final battle occurs, it will begin in Jerusalem, with the armies of the world gathering in the Holy City before heading to the Jezreel Valley.

At this point, Revelation 19:11 and following tells us that Jesus and the Christians who are with Him will get on white horses and return to the earth. And Jesus will descend upon the Mount of Olives in the city of Jerusalem, the eternal capital of the nation of Israel.

Following the Battle of Armageddon and the victorious return of Christ to the earth will be a 1,000-year period of time called the millennium. Revelation 20:1-10 tells us that during that 1,000-year period, Satan will be bound in a bottomless pit. Those who know Christ as Lord and Savior will rule and reign with Him for that 1,000-year period of time. At the end of the 1,000 years, Satan will be released for a season, then captured again by God. Then comes the Great White Throne Judgment, at which time Jesus Christ will stand as judge (Revelation 20:11-15). Those who have rejected Him will be sentenced to eternity in the lake of fire, which is the "second death." After that will come eternity future—a new heaven, a new earth, and a new Jerusalem (Revelation 21–22).

## The Satanic Trinity

During the Tribulation, there will be what some call the satanic Trinity. In the end times, this satanic Trinity will do everything possible to replicate the holy Trinity. God the Father, God the Son, and God the Holy Spirit comprise the holy Trinity. By contrast Satan, or the devil, as he's defined in Revelation, will try to replicate God the Father. The second member of the satanic Trinity is the beast found in Revelation 13:1. He is mentioned 42 times in the rest of the book of Revelation. This is a reference to the Antichrist. In fact, the Antichrist has 27 names mentioned throughout Scripture. One name given to him is "Beast coming up out of the sea" (NASB). Third, there is the false prophet of Revelation 13:12 and following. He will attempt to replicate the ministry of the Holy Spirit.

## The Outline of Revelation

At the beginning of the book of Revelation, Jesus gave His own outline for the book to the apostle John. In Revelation 1:19, we learn that Jesus told John: "Write the things which you have seen" (NASB). This is the vision of Jesus, the power and the person of Jesus Christ. He then explains "the things which are" (NASB), a statement which refers to the letters to the seven churches in Revelation 2 and 3. Third, Jesus commands John to write "the things which will take place after these things" (NASB), which refers to future events. So Revelation covers the three time periods: the past (chapter 1), the present (chapters 2–3, the time of John's writing), and the future (chapters 4–22). We turn next to the future events described in chapters 4–22.

# Chapter 12

# THE RAPTURE, THE RETURN OF CHRIST, AND THE RETRIBUTION

In our last chapter, we introduced the three pillars that form our framework for understanding the book of Revelation. These three pillars represent the three main events on God's calendar of activities that are laid out for us in Revelation.

The first pillar begins in Revelation 4:1. The rapture of the church will happen at this point. Jesus will shout, the voice of the archangel will be heard, the trumpet of God will sound, and we will be caught up to be with Him. After that will come seven years of terrible judgment upon the earth, a time referred to as the Tribulation.

The second pillar represents the return of Christ back to the earth—the revelation of Jesus Christ. At the second coming, Jesus Christ will descend upon the Mount of Olives in the city of Jerusalem. He will defeat His enemies and then begin His 1,000-year millenial reign. Satan will be bound during those 1,000 years. Jesus Christ will begin a theocracy, ruling and reigning over His kingdom.

The third pillar (and the last of the three main events that we see in the book of Revelation) is the Great White Throne Judgment. That's when Jesus Christ will sentence those whose names are not written in the book of life, and they will be sent to the lake of fire. Satan, the Antichrist, and the false prophet will also be cast there. After that, those who are believers will experience eternity future—a new heaven, a new earth, and a new Jerusalem.

## The Jesus of the Book of Revelation

At the very beginning of the book of Revelation, the apostle John describes the person of Jesus Christ. What does Jesus reveal about Himself?

Many people think about only one aspect of Christ—they view Him as the meek and mild Jesus who was led away and crucified without saying a word. But Jesus Christ, as seen by John the Revelator, is returning to earth as the judge of all humanity. Revelation chapter 1 describes Jesus' white hair, depicting His purity and longevity. We are told He has eyes like flames of fire. The Bible talks frequently about Jesus Christ being able to see everything that occurs on earth. His voice is as the sound of many waters. It was His voice that spoke the worlds into existence, and it is His voice that will shout and call Christians to be with Him at the rapture of the church. And it is this same voice that will say to many, "I never knew you. Depart from Me into everlasting hell and damnation" (see Matthew 7:23).

Jesus' feet are described as fine brass, as if they had been burned in a furnace. His face shines brightly as the sun in its very strength. And, of course, He has the seven stars in His right hand, He is walking among seven golden candlesticks. Revelation 1:20 explains that the seven stars are the seven angels of the seven churches, and the seven golden candlesticks are the seven churches themselves. All this describes Jesus standing as a judge among His churches.

Jesus said, in Revelation 1:18, "I am the First and the Last. I am the Living One." This talks about the fact that Jesus Christ has life in Himself that He can give to anybody. Revelation 1:18 is the cornerstone of our faith; Jesus shared His testimony in this verse: "I was dead, and behold I am alive for ever and ever!" That proves that He was who He said He was. He rose from the dead and is now alive.

Revelation 1:18 confirms Jesus can do what He said He is going to do. He can give life to all because of His resurrection. That is not only the cornerstone of our faith, it is also the foundation of Bible prophecy. The resurrected Jesus Christ is the only one qualified to tell us what's going to happen in the future. And that is, in fact, exactly what He does when He says to John, "Write, therefore, what you have seen, what is now and what will take place later" (Revelation 1:19).

The last words of Jesus Christ to the church aren't found in the Gospels or in the letters of Paul. They are found in Revelation. He sent seven letters to seven actual churches, and these letters also apply to the body of Christ today.

## Lessons from the Seven Churches

Specifically, Jesus speaks to the "angel" of each of these churches. "Angel" in the original Greek language is *angelos*. It's not a pastor or human messenger. It's specifically an angel at each church. Jesus gives a message to each of these angels, which is preceded by the description of Himself from chapter 1. He says, "I know your works." That is, He has been watching what they do. Remember, His eyes are as a flame of fire. He is able to see every single thing His people do.

Look at what Jesus said to the church of Smyrna in Revelation 2:9: "I know your afflictions and your poverty." To the church at Sardis He said, "I know your deeds, that you have a reputation of being alive, but you are dead" (3:1). To the church at Philadelphia He said, "I know that you have little strength. But you have kept my word and have not denied my name" (Revelation 3:8). It is important to realize that Jesus Christ knew what was happening in each of these churches. But how does that apply to us today?

Note that Jesus condemned five of the churches He wrote to. On the other hand, He commends two of the churches—the church at

Smyrna and the church at Philadelphia. Those in the Philadelphia church were said to have little strength, but because they stood upon the authority of the Word of God, they could reach the world for Jesus Christ. But to the church at Laodicea, Jesus said, "Because you are lukewarm—neither hot nor cold—I am about to spit you out of My mouth" (Revelation 3:16).

## THE SEVEN CHURCHES OF REVELATION

| CHURCH | CHARACTER | COMPROMISE | CHALLENGE | COMMITMENT |
|---|---|---|---|---|
| Ephesus (2:1-7) | Hard work, patient endurance, rejected evil, persevered | Left their first love | Repent and do what you did at first | You will eat from the truth of life |
| Smyrna (2:8-11) | Endured suffering and poverty | None | Remain faithful despite persecution | I will give you the crown of life; you will not be hurt by the second death |
| Pergamum (2:12-17) | Loyalty to Christ | Blending of religions, false teaching, idolatry, immorality | Repent | Given hidden manna and a stone with a new name on it |
| Thyatira (2:18-29) | Love, faith, actions, endurance, improvement | Blending of religions, idolatry, immorality | Repent | Authority over nations and gift of the morning star |
| Sardis (3:1-6) | Only a remnant have stayed faithful; others are spiritually dead | They are dead | Strengthen the little faith that remains | The faithful will walk with Christ and not be removed from book of life |
| Philadelphia (3:7-13) | Kept Christ's word and did not deny Him | None | Christ gave them an open door; He would keep them from the hour of trial | I will make you a pillar in the temple of My God |
| Laodicea (3:14-22) | None | Lukewarm, neither hot nor cold | Repent from apathy | I will invite those who overcome to sit with Me on My throne |

Chart courtesy of Dillon Burroughs, 2009.

What Christ said in the seven letters can also be applied to churches today and to each of us personally. Jesus was saying, "Wake up! Here's where we are. Here's what I know about you." He was telling people to turn around, turn away from sin, and go the other direction: "If you don't repent, I will remove your candlestick." Our Lord concluded by saying, "He who has an ear, let him hear." He said this to all seven churches, and the message is for Christians today as well.

## The Overcomers

Jesus then talks in Revelation, on nine separate occasions, about those who are overcomers. Seven of these occurrences are in chapters 2 and 3 (2:7,11,17,26; 3:5,12,21). The remaining two occur regarding Christ overcoming His enemies (17:14) and the inheritance of overcomers (21:7). According to 1 John 5:4, an overcomer is someone who knows Jesus Christ as their Lord and Savior. John writes, "Everyone who believes that Jesus is the Christ is born of God" (1 John 5:1). Then he says, "Everyone born of God overcomes the world" (verse 4). To overcome the world is to gain victory over its sinful pattern of life, which is another way of describing obedience to God. Such obedience is possible for believers because they have been born again, and the Holy Spirit dwells within them and gives them strength.

Jesus made some wonderful promises to those who are overcomers. In Revelation 2:7, Jesus said, "To him who overcomes, I will give you the right to eat from the tree of life, which is in the midst of the paradise of God." That promise was not only for the seven historical churches in Asia Minor, but also for the people in the churches we have today. That's why Revelation 2 and 3 are so important. They will bring revival and renewal to anyone who will spend time in these two chapters.

## The Rapture, the Hope of the Church

Revelation marks the point of the rapture, the first of our three pillars under discussion. This doctrine is spelled out in numerous passages.

For example, the apostle Paul wrote, "Listen, I tell you a mystery: We will not all sleep, but we will all be changed—in a flash, in the twinkling of an eye, at the last trumpet. For the trumpet will sound, the dead will be raised imperishable, and we will be changed" (1 Corinthians 15:51-52). Paul taught us four things in that passage.

First, he said he would reveal a new truth: "Listen, I tell you a mystery." This mystery was something not previously known, but now revealed. The new truth was not that the Lord would return to earth. It was not about the future resurrection of the dead. Believers in the Old Testament already knew these truths. So what was the new truth? It includes the second, third, and fourth things Paul mentioned in 1 Corinthians 15:51-52:

The second thing Paul tells us is that not all Christians will have to die to go to heaven. That is, "we will not all sleep." Sometime in the future the rapture will take place and a whole generation of believers will be taken en masse into God's presence. Those Christians will never know what it is to die physically.

Third, Paul said, "We shall all be changed—in a flash, in the twinkling of an eye." When the rapture happens, all Christians will be changed. The Greek word *allasso* literally means "to be transformed." Believers who are alive will be instantly given new immortal bodies—that is, spiritual bodies like the Lord Jesus. These bodies will never get sick, never sin, and never die.

Fourth, how long will it take for our bodies to be changed? Paul said, "We will all be changed—in a flash, in the twinkling of an eye, at the last trumpet. For the trumpet will sound, the dead will be raised imperishable, and we will be changed." Someone has estimated that "the twinkling of an eye" takes about one-thousandth of a second. The Greek word for "flash" is *atomos,* from which we get the word *atom.* It refers to a period of time so small it cannot be divided. The twinkling of an eye does not refer to how fast a person blinks, but how fast light can flash on or across the pupil—that fast, and faster.

To another church, Paul wrote,

> This we say to you by the word of the Lord, that we who are alive and remain until the coming of the Lord, will not precede those who have fallen asleep. For the Lord Himself will descend from heaven with a shout, with the voice of the archangel and with the trumpet of God, and the dead in Christ will rise first. Then we who are alive and remain will be caught up [raptured] together with them in the clouds to meet the Lord in the air, and so we shall always be with the Lord. Therefore comfort one another with these words (1 Thessalonians 4:15-18 NASB).

In the flash of a second, every living believer on the earth will be changed and given an immortal body that will never die. This is the rapture—when Jesus Christ suddenly comes to catch up Christians all over the world, and He will do so without warning. Only unbelievers will be left populating the earth.

Jesus Himself taught that He would someday come back for believers. He said, "Let not your heart be troubled; you believe in God, believe also in Me. In My Father's house are many mansions; if it were not so, I would have told you. I go to prepare a place for you. And if I go and prepare a place for you, I will come again and receive you to Myself; that where I am, there you may be also" (John 14:1-3 NKJV).

Jesus stated five points in those words: First, He said "In my Father's house are many mansions." The Father's house is a specific location—heaven. Second, Jesus said, "I go to prepare a place for you." The place He is preparing for us is in heaven. Third, He said, "I will come again." Jesus Himself said He will return in the future. Fourth, Jesus said He will come to take us to be with Him. This can only refer to the rapture—Paul wrote, "The Lord Himself will descend from heaven with a shout, with the voice of the archangel and with the trumpet of God, and the dead in Christ will rise first. Then we who are alive and remain shall be caught up together with them in the clouds to meet the Lord in the air" (1 Thessalonians 4:16-17 NASB). Fifth, where did Jesus say He will take us? "I will come again and receive you to Myself; that where

I am, there you may be also" (NKJV). Jesus is in heaven now preparing a place for us. When He comes and receives us to Himself, Jesus will take us to that place in heaven—His Father's house.

## The Analogy of the Rapture to the Jewish Marriage Tradition

When Jesus said, "If I go and prepare a place for you, I will come again and *receive* you to Myself," He used a verb ("receive") that, in the New Testament, is usually used to describe the action of a bride-groom taking his betrothed wife unto himself. It is the same word we find in Matthew 1:20, where Joseph was told, "Do not be afraid *to tak*e Mary home as your wife," or in Matthew 1:24, where it says, "When Joseph woke up, he did what the angel of the Lord had commanded him and *took* Mary home as his wife." "To take" in this verse is the same word Jesus used when He said, "I will come again and *receive* you to Myself" (NKJV).

Why did Jesus use the same word? It appears Jesus was implying an analogy between the Jewish marriage customs in Bible times and His coming to receive His bride, the church.

How did a Jewish couple become married? The groom would leave his father's home and travel to the home of his prospective bride. By analogy, Jesus left His Father's house in heaven over 2,000 years ago and traveled to the home of His prospective bride, the church, here on earth.

In Bible times, a Jewish groom would establish a marriage covenant by paying a tribute or purchase price to the wife's family. By analogy, when Jesus came in His first coming to earth, He also came to establish a covenant by which He would obtain His bride. The Bible calls this the new covenant.

Jesus established the new covenant when He died on the cross and paid the purchase price necessary to obtain His bride, the church. The purchase price Jesus had to pay was the shedding of His own life's blood. Paul said in 1 Corinthians 6:19-20, "Know ye not that your body is the temple of the Holy Ghost which is in you, which ye have of God, and ye are not your own? For ye are bought with a price: therefore glorify God in your body, and in your spirit, which are God's" (KJV).

After a Jewish groom established the marriage covenant, he would promise to return before leaving his bride at her home and go back to his father's house. They would remain separated for a period of time, normally about a year. By analogy, less than two months after Jesus established the new covenant through the shedding of His blood on the cross of Calvary, He promised He would return and left the home of His prospective bride (the church here on the earth) and returned on the day of His ascension to His Father's house in heaven.

During the year of separation, the Jewish groom would stay at his father's house to build living accommodations for him and his future bride. According to John 14, after Jesus had established the new covenant, He left His bride on earth and went to His Father's house in heaven, where He has been busily engaged in preparing living accommodations or mansions to which He will later bring His bride, the church.

The Jewish bridegroom, at the end of the year of separation, would come on an unannounced night to take his bride to be with him. The Jewish bridegroom would come only after he had finished preparing the living quarters to which he would bring his new bride (and after his father gave his approval).

By analogy, the Bible teaches that at the end of the present separation of Christ from His bride, Jesus will come from the Father's house in heaven to the home of His bride here on earth at an unannounced time. In Mark 13:32 Jesus taught, "No one knows about that day or hour, not even the angels in heaven, nor the Son, but only the Father. Be on guard! Be alert! You do not know when that time will come."

When the Jewish bridegroom came on the unannounced night, he and his male escorts would wait outside the bride's home until she was ready. By analogy, Paul tells us in 1 Thessalonians 4, when Jesus comes for His bride, the church, He will not come the whole way down to the earth where His bride is living. He will stop above the earth, in the air, and wait there until the church comes up to meet Him.

After the Jewish bride came out of her home, the couple would return together by torchlight procession back to the groom's father's house. By analogy, after Jesus has caught up the church from the earth to meet Him in the air, He will return with His bride to His Father's house in heaven to begin living in the accommodations He has prepared there.

After the Jewish bride and groom arrived at the groom's father's house, they went into a room that the Jewish people called *hupa*. They would stay hidden in that bridal chamber for seven days, in what was known as "the seven days of the bridal chamber." At the end of the seventh day, the groom would come out of hiding with his bride, with her veil removed, so that everyone could see his bride. By analogy, after Jesus and His bride arrive at His Father's house in heaven, He and His bride will go into hiding for a period of seven years. During that time, the seven-year Tribulation period will be transpiring on earth. At the end of the seven-year Tribulation, Christ will come out of hiding from the Father's house in heaven in His glorious second coming, and come all the way down to the earth to rule over it on behalf of God. He will bring His bride with Him in full public display so that everyone can see who His bride truly is.

## Five Reasons Christians Will Not Go Through the Tribulation

Some people ask, Will Christians experience any part of the Tribulation? We believe there are at least five biblical reasons Christians—or the church—will not go through any part of the Tribulation period.

First, in 1 Thessalonians 4:13-18, the apostle Paul wrote to correct some Christians who were afraid that they had missed the rapture and therefore would have to live through the terrible Tribulation period. Paul assured them they had not missed the rapture and were not living in the day of the Lord's judgment. The very fact that these Christians were afraid they were living in the time of the Lord's judgment and had missed the rapture proves that Paul taught them that the rapture would occur before the Tribulation.

A second reason Christians will not go through the Tribulation is based on comparing John 14:1-3 and 1 Thessalonians 4:17 with Zechariah 14:4. John 14:1-3 teaches Jesus is in heaven preparing a place for us; He is going to come back and "receive us to Himself" and take us "to the Father's house" (NASB). First Thessalonians 4:17 agrees, stating that when Christ comes back from heaven, He won't come all the way down to the earth. Christ will come *for* His church and meet them *in the air*. By contrast, Zechariah 14:4 says that at the second coming, the saints will come down from heaven to the earth with Christ to fight Antichrist and the armies of the world and to rescue Israel, and to rule with Christ on earth in His millennial kingdom. We see in the above verses two phases of Christ's coming: first, the rapture, when Christ comes and believers meet Him in the air, and second, after the Tribulation, Christ's second coming, when He comes to the earth to rule.

Third, the Bible specifically teaches that Christians will not go through the Tribulation, but be delivered from the wrath to come. In 1 Thessalonians 1:9-10, the apostle Paul wrote, "You turned to God from idols to serve the living and true God, and to wait for His Son from heaven, whom He raised from the dead, even Jesus who delivers us from the wrath to come" (NKJV). The word "rescues" refers to deliverance by a mighty act of power. The rapture will certainly be a mighty act of power, because Jesus will call up to Himself all believers on the earth from all the centuries that the church has existed. Christians who are alive at the time of the rapture will instantly be changed; their bodies will be transformed into immortal bodies and snatched from the earth to meet Christ in the air and be taken to the Father's house in heaven. Further, when Paul says Christians will be delivered from "the coming wrath," the Greek text literally says "the wrath, the coming." Greek scholars say the word "the" is used twice because Paul is referring to a very specific, distinctive period of wrath that is unique to all of history—the seven-year Tribulation. Christians will be delivered from the wrath to come.

Fourth, as we have already mentioned, Revelation 3:10 promises the church will be kept from the hour of trial that is to come upon the whole world: "Because you have kept my commandment to persevere, I also will keep you from the hour of trial which shall come upon the whole world, to test those who dwell on the earth" (NKJV). Jesus will keep Christians out of the Tribulation.

Fifth, in the book of Revelation, the church is not identified as being on earth during the Tribulation. On the other hand, the church is mentioned 19 times in Revelation chapters 1–3. But from Revelation 4:1 to Revelation 19—the Tribulation chapters of the book of Revelation—the church vanishes completely from earth and is not mentioned once. Why? The answer can only be that the church is not present on earth; it has been raptured and delivered from the wrath to come.

## When Will the Judgment Seat of Christ Occur?

First Corinthians 15 says that in "the twinkling of an eye," believers will be instantly transformed, and given new, immortal bodies, and be snatched or caught up from earth to meet Christ in the air. Then Jesus will take us back to the Father's house in heaven. It is then that Christians will stand before the judgment seat of Christ in preparation for the marriage supper of the Lamb. Revelation describes believers as wearing wedding garments, and the marriage ceremony is described in Revelation 19:7-9. The marriage supper of the Lamb is an event and celebration that will last all through the seven years of the Tribulation.

Between the rapture and the beginning of the Tribulation period is a short time during which the judgment seat of Christ will take place. We don't know how long this time is, and this judgment does not determine who enters heaven and who does not. A person will not stand at the judgment seat of Christ unless he or she is saved. This will be a time when the works of believers will be judged so that rewards can be given to those who faithfully served Christ. There will be some good works that will receive eternal rewards, and there will be some actions that will cause us to suffer loss.

What are the rewards Christians can receive at the judgment seat of Christ? The Bible speaks of five distinct crowns:

1. First, there is the crown incorruptible (1 Corinthians 9:25).
2. Second, there is the crown of rejoicing for being a soul winner (1 Thessalonians 2:19).
3. Third, there is a crown of life for not yielding to temptation (James 1:12).
4. Fourth, there is a crown of glory for helping the body of Christ to grow (1 Peter 5:1-4).
5. Fifth, there is a crown of righteousness that Paul said he would receive, but not him only, but all of us who eagerly anticipate the coming of Jesus Christ (2 Timothy 4:8).

In Revelation 4:10, we read that believers will take their crowns and will lay them at Jesus' feet in thanksgiving for what He did for them. Though the crowns are thrown at Christ's feet, the rewards that accompany them will continue on for all eternity.

It is also at the judgment seat of Christ that the garments or clothing believers wear, signifying the kinds of works they did, will be given to them for the marriage supper of the Lamb.

## After the Rapture

As we once again come to Revelation 4:1, we see a transition marking the rapture of the church. The church is made up of both Jews and Gentiles who have come to know Jesus Christ as Lord and Savior during this current church age. The verse tells us that there was a door opened in heaven. John the Revelator spoke of the voice like a trumpet talking with him, and it said, "Come up here, and I will show you what must take place after this." Immediately, John was in the presence of God in the heavenly throne room. This is when the church is taken away from the earth, leaving two groups of people on the earth—Gentiles and Jews.

Revelation 4:1 is the first of the three main events in Revelation that tells of a time in history when the rapture takes place. In the Upper Room the night before Jesus was crucified, He told His disciples that He was going to heaven to "prepare a place" for them and that He would come back to take them where He was going (John 14:1-3).

When John mentioned "the first voice which I had heard, like the sound of a trumpet speaking with me" (Revelation 4:1 NASB), it reminds us of the Scripture Paul had written pertaining to the rapture in 1 Thessalonians 4:13-18 and 1 Corinthians 15:51-53, where he spoke of a trumpet sound that will be part of the procedure for the rapture.

The church consists of Christians, Gentiles, and Jews who receive Jesus as their Lord and Savior during the time between the day of Pentecost in Acts 2 and the rapture, which is known as the church age. The only ones left on earth after the rapture will be unbelieving Jews and Gentiles who enter the "time of testing," the seven-year-long Tribulation period. During the next sixteen chapters of the book of Revelation, the Tribulation period is played out. It's a time when the Lord will deal with Israel, which will come under fire from the Gentile world powers who desire to destroy the Jewish people.

## Israel's Role In the Tribulation

At this time in history, God will continue the program that He had started in the Old Testament for the Jewish people, moving to fulfill the covenants that He gave them. This includes the Abrahamic covenant first revealed in Genesis 15:18-21, which guaranteed that the Jews would be a nation of people among the nations of the world. In verse 18, we read, "On the same day the LORD made a covenant with Abram, saying: 'To your descendants I have given this land'" (NASB).

There are 38 different passages in the Bible that give the biblical borders of Israel. A compilation of these 38 passages of the land God has promised to give them would indicate the Jewish people will ultimately be given one half of modern-day Egypt, all of Israel, Lebanon, Syria, Jordan, and Kuwait, three-fourths of Iraq, and three-fourths of Saudi Arabia. This is a prophecy that will be fulfilled in what is called the kingdom period, when Jesus sets up the millennial kingdom. This land covenant, described in Deuteronomy 30, is the guarantee of that land being given to the Jews. The Davidic covenant in 2 Samuel 7 promises the Jewish people that there will be a Jewish descendant of King David who will rule from a temple on the Temple Mount in the city of Jerusalem. Both covenants will be fulfilled after the seven-year Tribulation, a time of judgment on the Jews.

In Revelation chapters 4–19, we are given detailed information about the Tribulation period. The Jews will play a key role on this earth during a terrible time of judgment also referred to as the time of "Jacob's trouble" by the prophet Jeremiah (Jeremiah 30:7 KJV). In Revelation 5, we see a heavenly scene of the throne room of God in heaven. God the Father has a sealed book in His hand—a book that could also be called the "title deed" to the earth. God has promised that His Son Jesus will receive a kingdom, the kingdom ultimately promised to the Jewish people. The promise in Daniel 7:13-14 says the "Ancient of Days," God the Father, will give the Son of Man, Jesus Christ, a kingdom and a dominion that will last forever. That kingdom is the thousand-year period of time called the millennium, which will come after the seven years of tribulation. Returning to chapter 5, we see the sealed book in the hand of God the Father. Someone asks, "Who is worthy to break the seals and open the scroll?" Then one of the 24 elders says, "Why not Jesus? He was pure, perfect, and without sin." That's a paraphrase of what he actually said: "Weep not: behold, the Lion of Juda, the Root of David, hath prevailed to open the book, and to loose the seven seals thereof" (Revelation 5:5 KJV). This title deed to the earth is for the purpose of allowing Jesus Christ and God the Father to bring the people of the earth under His submission. This is so that the kingdom promised to the Jewish people with Jesus Christ as the King of kings and Lord of lords can be set up on the earth.

Because of this fact, Israel will come under fire due to the activities of Satan. The Satanic trinity (made up of Satan, the Antichrist, and the false prophet) will try to annihilate the Jewish people so that God's promise to them will not be fulfilled. We see this struggle unveiled in these 16 chapters of Revelation (chapters 4–19), which deal with this time of testing, the time of Jacob's trouble—the Tribulation period. During that time of testing, there will be two peoples of the human family that will be on earth: Jews and Gentiles. At the rapture, Christians will leave the earth and go into heaven into the presence of Jesus Christ forever (1 Thessalonians 4:17). That leaves only Gentiles and Jews on the earth. There are approximately twelve million Jews on the earth at this time in history, and they will play a key role in God's plan during the following Tribulation period.

There are three purposes for the Tribulation period: One is to evangelize Jews, giving each and every Jew the opportunity to receive Jesus Christ as their Lord and Savior. The second purpose, as foretold in the book of Daniel (chapters 2 and 7), will be to bring an end to the Gentile world powers who will be ruling the earth at this time under the leadership of the Antichrist. The third reason for the Tribulation period is to bring an end to the Satanic trinity of Satan, Antichrist, and the false prophet.

## The Antichrist and the Seven Seal Judgments

Then in chapter 6 of Revelation, we find the revealing of six of the seven sealed judgments. The first sealed judgment, found in 6:1-2, is a man on a white horse who comes forth wearing a crown on his head.

He has a bow in his hand without arrows and he goes forth conquering and to conquer. At first glance many people think that this may be Jesus Christ because He comes on a white horse back to the earth. Jesus Christ *does* come back to the earth on a white horse according to Revelation 19:11. However, Jesus comes back to earth on a white horse at the *end* of the Tribulation. Revelation 6:1-2, in contrast, occurs soon after the rapture in the beginning part of the Tribulation.

This individual on the white horse in Revelation 6:1-2, the first sealed judgment, is the one who would like to replicate Jesus Christ of the Holy Trinity. This is the Antichrist. The term *Antichrist* is given to an individual who will be energized by Satan according to Revelation 13:2, and is referred to by 27 other names in the Bible. The male Gentile who will be known as the Antichrist will be selected by Satan and his power and seat of authority will be given to this world dictator at the beginning of the Tribulation period.

Revelation 13 is a detailed passage of Scripture that deals with the Antichrist. Verse 2 tells us that the dragon is defined as Satan in Revelation 12:9, gives the Antichrist his power, his throne, and great authority. So the Antichrist, a false Messiah, comes on the scene early on in the seven-year Tribulation period. This Antichrist comes out of the Revived Roman Empire. One of his 27 names will be the "little horn" (see Daniel 7:8). The little horn comes out of the ten horns of Daniel 7:7-8, which is a prophecy depicting the Revived Roman Empire, which will come to power in the Tribulation period. This text confirms the Antichrist will be a Gentile.

The next question may be, "Why would the Jewish people accept a Gentile leader as their Messiah?" That is a great question, and it is answered by Paul in 2 Thessalonians 2:8-12, where we learn that those who reject the love of the truth will receive a strong delusion from God that they might believe the lie of Satan. There will be Jewish people in the Tribulation who will accept this "false Messiah" because they refused to believe in Jesus Christ, the true Messiah. The Antichrist will play a key role in the lives of the Jewish people on the earth during the

Tribulation period. When the Antichrist comes to power, he will go to the Middle East for the purpose of establishing a peace between the Jewish people and their Islamic-Arab neighbors, which are enemies to the Jewish nation in that region of the world.

The Antichrist, according to Daniel 9:27, will confirm a peace treaty with the Jewish people, which actually starts the clock ticking on the seven-year Tribulation period. Daniel 9:27 says he, that is, the Antichrist, will confirm a covenant with many. That covenant is a treaty with the Jewish people and their neighbors, lasting for one "week," a seven-year period.

This peace treaty is *confirmed*. It is not a signed peace treaty. What is very interesting is that the Bible does not say in any location that the Antichrist will sign a peace treaty. Rather, Daniel 9:27 says he will "confirm" a covenant.

There are three peace treaties that are already on the table with Israel and some of her neighbors. Currently, none of these treaties have been normalized. None of them are working.

## Peace Treaties

In 1979, President Jimmy Carter met with then Prime Minister of Israel Menachem Begin and then President of Egypt Anwar Sadat at Camp David, which is the retreat compound for the President of the United States in the state of Maryland.

These three world leaders forged together a treaty called the Camp David Accords, which was the first peace treaty between Israel and one of its neighbors, Egypt.

In September of 1993 there was another peace treaty that was signed between Israel and one of her neighbors. Then United States President Bill Clinton brought the Prime Minister of Israel at that time, Yitzhak Rabin, to the White House, along with the Chairman of the Palestinian Liberation Organization, Yasser Arafat. There they signed a peace treaty called the Oslo Accords.

This treaty was to bring peace between the Israelis and the Palestinians. But it too has never been normalized. Both the Camp David Accords and the Oslo Accords are treaties that have never been normalized and are waiting for somebody to strengthen them, make them stronger, or confirm them, as Daniel 9:27 says will be the case. (Here's something interesting to note: The word "confirm" in Daniel 9:27 is the Hebrew word *gabar*, which means to strengthen, to make stronger, or to confirm.)

There is also a third peace treaty that is on the table between the Israelis and one of her neighbors. In October of 1994, President Bill Clinton brought together the King of Jordan, King Hussein, and the late Prime Minister of Israel, Yitzhak Rabin. They signed the peace treaty between Israel and the Hashemite Kingdom of Jordan.

Here is a third peace treaty that is on the table, not working, waiting for somebody to confirm it and make it work. During the first part of the Tribulation, the Antichrist will appear and come into Israel to confirm this peace treaty—a pseudo, short-lived peace treaty between the Jewish people and their neighbors.

This will then cause the Jewish people to believe that their Messiah has arrived and delivered them, which results in their willingness to lay down their weapons and live without a major defense as they are today. They will rely upon what they believe to be their Messiah, the Antichrist, who will promise to protect and give security to the nation of Israel. After this time, the second sealed judgment found in Revelation 6:3-4 takes place. When the second seal is opened, this is what happens: "Then another horse came out, a fiery red one. Its rider was given power to take peace from the earth and to make men slay one another. To him was given a large sword" (verse 4).

This is the sealed judgment of war that will take place on the earth early in the first days of the Tribulation period. In order to understand this sealed judgment, we must look at Daniel 11:40-45, Ezekiel 38, and Psalm 83.

## Nations Aligned Against Israel

These three passages of Scripture give the names of the nations that will align themselves against the Jewish people in the last days. Their goal will be to wipe the Jewish people off of the face of the earth, that their name be forgotten forever.

One of the nations listed in this coalition of nations that will come against Israel in the last days is Persia, known today as Iran. President Ahmadinejad of Iran has made a statement about Israel that is almost a direct quote from Psalm 83:4, where it describes the leaders of this coalition of nations gathering together and coming out of their meeting, saying, "'Come,' they say, 'let us destroy them as a nation, that the name of Israel be remembered no more.'"

As we look at Daniel 11, Ezekiel 38, and Psalm 83, we can determine the nations that will align themselves against the Jewish state of Israel. In Daniel 11:40-45 we read about the "king of the north," defined earlier in chapter 11 as what we know as modern-day Syria, and the king of the south, as what we know as modern-day Egypt; these two nations will make the first move against the nation of Israel. In verse 40, it talks about the king of the south coming at him and the king of the north coming at him. The "him" in this passage of Scripture is a pronoun used to describe the person of the Antichrist. You may ask, "How will Egypt and Syria come against him?" It can be explained by understanding that the Antichrist has confirmed a peace treaty between Israel and its neighbors.

The Antichrist has given a guarantee to protect the Jewish people as their Messiah, even though he is a false Messiah. When the two nations, Syria in the north and Egypt in the south, attack Israel, they will in effect be attacking the Antichrist and his territory. The Antichrist, according to Revelation 17, will be located in the city of Rome, where he will be establishing a one-world religious operation, the Ecclesiastical Babylon. In Daniel 11:41, the Antichrist will hear the news and come rushing into the "glorious land," which is Israel.

Antichrist will destroy Syria in the north. Then he will come down through Amman, Moab, and Edom, but will not touch Jordan. Amman, Moab, and Edom are the biblical names for the three parts of what we know as modern-day Jordan.

The reason for this is that Petra, a place that God has prepared to protect the Jewish people during at least the last three-and-a-half years of the Tribulation period, cannot be harmed. The Antichrist will make his way through Jordan, will go to the south, destroy Egypt, turn around, start back toward Jerusalem, and according to Daniel 11:43, the Libyans and Ethiopians will be at his steps.

The Libyans would be the people referred to as Put (or Libya) in Ezekiel 38:5. They are the people under the current leadership of Colonel Khadafi. Ethiopia would be "Cush" in the Hebrew terminology, which would include the three nations of Ethiopia, Somalia, and Sudan. They will be at the steps of the Antichrist when he makes his way back toward Jerusalem. But then Daniel 11:44 talks about reports coming out of the east and out of the north that will alarm the Antichrist. In order to determine the nations out of the east and north, we need to go over to Ezekiel 38.

In Ezekiel 38, the ancient Jewish prophet Ezekiel prophesies about the Battle of Gog and Magog. In 38:2, we see Gog mentioned. Gog will be the person in the leadership role in this battle in the land of Magog. Magog, of course, is the location of one of the nations that will align themselves against the Jewish nation of Israel. Also in verse 2, we see Meshech and Tubal. Looking down to verse 6, we find Gomer and Togarmah.

There is a hermeneutical principle in biblical geography. Who was the author writing about when he wrote the book? What geographical area did they live in? When Ezekiel wrote chapter 38, he mentioned the names of Magog, Meshech, Tubal, Gomer, and Togarmah, and then in verse 5, Persia, Ethiopia, and Libya. The people living in these geographical areas in the future will form a coalition to try to wipe the Jewish nation off the face of the earth, and bring Israel under fire. In order to determine who these nations are today, we have to go back to Genesis 9.

After the flood in Genesis 9:1, God told Noah and those on the ark to be fruitful, multiply, and repopulate the earth. In Genesis 10, we see the beginning of the obedience of the sons of Noah, having children and endeavoring to repopulate the earth. Notice in Genesis 10:2 that the sons of Japheth included Gomer and Magog. Then you skip a couple and find Tubal and Meshech. Then in verse 3, you find Togarmah. This is describing a group of Noah's grandsons, the sons of Japheth. Notice verse 5: "From these the coastland peoples of the Gentiles were separated into their lands, everyone according to his language, according to their families, into their nations" (NKJV). These grandsons of Noah went to a location geographically to establish their families and then a nation. They would even develop the language they would be speaking.

Magog, according to authorities, would be the area north of the Caspian and Black Sea, which is modern-day Russia. Meshech, Tubal, Gomer, and Togarmah would be in biblical times the four geographical areas of what we know as modern-day Turkey.

Ezekiel 38:5 mentions Persia. Until 1936, there were three nations known as Persia, which today would be Afghanistan, Pakistan, and Iran. In addition to Persia, Ezekiel mentions Ethiopia, which is modern-day Ethiopia, Somalia, and Sudan, and Libya, which is modern-day Libya. These are some of the nations that will be a part of the coalition that will go against the nation of Israel. There are also two other nations we should notice. Psalm 83:6 talks about the Ishmaelites. Ishmael went to live in the area of Arabia that is Saudi Arabia today. Recognize that in verse 7, Tyre is modern-day Lebanon.

According to Ezekiel, a coalition of nations living in these geographical areas will align themselves in the last days, against the nation of Israel, bringing Israel under fire. As we consider the interviews that we have written about earlier in this book, you can see how these nations have been making preparations over the years and are now ready to form this coalition to destroy the Jewish State of Israel.

The timing of this attack by this coalition of nations against the

Jewish State of Israel is determined by Ezekiel 38 (verses 8 and 11). Verse 8 talks about a time in the latter years when the Jewish people have been "brought out from among the nations, and now all of them live in safety." But according to verses 10-12, this situation will not last long:

> Thus says the Lord GOD: "On that day it shall come to pass that thoughts will arise in your mind, and you will make an evil plan: You will say, 'I will go up against a land of unwalled villages; I will go to a peaceful people, who dwell safely, all of them dwelling without walls, and having neither bars nor gates'—to take plunder and to take booty, to stretch out your hand against the waste places that are again inhabited, and against a people gathered from the nations, who have acquired livestock and goods, who dwell in the midst of the land" (NKJV).

This is military terminology. It is talking about the defense used during the time Ezekiel wrote this passage of Scripture. At that time, people would have had a wall around their city. They would not have had F-16s, nor tanks, nor Apache helicopters, but a wall around their city to defend themselves.

So when the prophet Ezekiel writes about living in unwalled villages, it means that the people living in those villages have laid down their defenses. Today it would refer to the Jewish people laying down their military power and trusting a world leader to protect them. But they are mistaken. Instead, this Antichrist will allow these nations, when there is this pseudopeace in place, to attack this Jewish State of Israel.

According to Scripture, Israel will be under fire when the second sealed judgment, the judgment of a man on a red horse of war, comes forth to conquer and to kill many with the sword.

At the Battle of Gog and Magog, this coalition of nations trying to wipe the Jewish State of Israel off the face of the earth will themselves be destroyed by God. But the Antichrist will usurp this victory from God, who will defeat this coalition of nations, according to Ezekiel 39:2. As a result of this battle, the Islamic world will be rendered inoperative.

## The Abomination of Desolation

This will happen in order for the Antichrist to be able to put together a false religion, which will be headquartered in the city of Rome in the first three-and-a-half years of the Tribulation period (see Revelation 17).

This Antichrist will usurp the victory from God given to the Jewish people. In Daniel 11:45, we are told that the Antichrist will go about setting up the location of his tabernacles: We can imagine him saying, "Plant the tabernacles of my palace between the seas in the glorious holy mountain." Now we are talking about the Antichrist giving the Jewish people the go-ahead to put up their temple on the "glorious holy mountain" (KJV)—the Temple Mount in Jerusalem.

The "glorious holy mountain" is a phrase used 18 times in the Scripture and always refers to the Temple Mount in the city of Jerusalem. When it talks about "between the seas," we are talking about between the Sea of Galilee in the north and the Red Sea in the south, in the east the Dead Sea and in the west the Mediterranean Sea.

Placed right between these four seas is the city of Jerusalem, where the Temple Mount is located. The Antichrist gives permission for the Jewish people to put their temple up. When the temple is erected in Jerusalem, then Israel will begin to see the events of the time of Jacob's trouble, Israel under fire.

Concerning this temple, Revelation 11:1 tells us John is given a reed to measure the location for the temple. This Jewish temple has to be standing on the Temple Mount in the city of Jerusalem at the midway point of the Tribulation. Why? Because the Antichrist will walk into the temple, into the Holy of Holies (see 2 Thessalonians 2:4), sit down, and claim to be God.

This is also referred to as the abomination of desolation that is spoken of by Daniel the prophet in Daniel 9:27, confirmed by Jesus Christ (Matthew 24:15), the apostle Paul (2 Thessalonians 2:4), and the apostle John (Revelation 11:1).

We have already discussed the plans by many today who are preparing to build this temple. According to biblical prophecy, the Jewish people will erect their temple on the Temple Mount in this city of Jerusalem. Also during the first three-and-a-half years of the Tribulation period, according to Revelation 11:3 and following, there will be two witnesses who will preach from the Temple Mount in the city of Jerusalem.

## The Two Witnesses

These two witnesses will have an effective ministry, which will result in 144,000 male virgin Jews coming to know Jesus Christ as their Lord and Savior at the beginning of the seven-year Tribulation period (Revelation 7:4-8).

These male virgin Jews will be sealed and protected for the seven-year Tribulation period, according to Revelation 7:3. They will have a ministry of preaching the "gospel of the kingdom" (Matthew 24:14) to every single person on the earth, giving an opportunity to both Jews and Gentiles to receive Jesus Christ as their Lord and Savior.

The identity of these two witnesses who will preach from the Temple Mount in the city of Jerusalem in the first three-and-a-half years of the Tribulation period (or a period of 1,260 days as referred to in Revelation 11:3) has been a matter of great speculation.

According to Malachi 4:5, Elijah is to be one of these witnesses because the text calls for Elijah to return and be the forerunner of the Messiah, Jesus Christ, during the Tribulation period before the great and dreadful day of the Lord comes.

The other witness could possibly be Enoch, a Gentile referred to in Genesis 5:21-24 as a man who walked on the earth and then walked with God into the heavens, having never died.

These are the only two men in history who lived upon the earth and went directly to heaven without dying. They will come back, minister for the three-and-a-half years during the Tribulation period, and then the Bible says that they will be killed.

Revelation 11:9 says that they will lie in the streets of Jerusalem for three-and-a-half days, their bodies not being put in the graves. Verse 10 says that those who dwell upon the earth will rejoice over their deaths and celebrate by sending gifts to one another because these two prophets had tormented those who lived on the earth.

But then, John the Revelator reveals to us that there will be a shout from heaven (verse 12): "Come up here." And these two witnesses will be resurrected and taken up to heaven while their enemies watch. The information about the two witnesses reveals God's plan for the Jewish people during the Tribulation period. He wants them to recognize that Jesus is the Messiah and come to know Him as their Lord and Savior. The ministry of these two witnesses results in the salvation of 144,000 male virgin Jewish men, 12,000 from each of the 12 tribes of Israel (Revelation 7:4-8; 14:1-4). Then these Jewish evangelists will preach the "gospel of the kingdom" to every soul on the earth throughout the seven-year Tribulation period (Matthew 24:14).

Indeed there will be a number of Jewish people that will turn to the Lord (Revelation 7:9), a group that no person can number. But we are also told that many of these will be martyred during the Tribulation period according to the fifth sealed judgment (Revelation 6:9).

## The Worst Holocaust of All Time

The fifth sealed judgment is martyrdom of believers, not Christians from the church age. Remember, Christians will have departed this earth at the rapture of the church before the Tribulation period begins.

But Jews and Gentiles who become believers during the Tribulation will be martyred for their testimony for standing for Jesus Christ.

In fact, the ancient Jewish prophet Zechariah says that during this time of testing, two out of every three Jews will be killed (Zechariah 13:8). At the present Jewish population in our world, that would be something in the area of over 8 million Jews. This will be the worst holocaust to ever take place upon the face of the earth. All of these prophecies will come to their fulfillment as the Jewish people come under fire during the Tribulation period.

A number of things will take place at the midway point of the Tribulation. Daniel 9:27 tells us that at that midway point (three-and-a-half years into the seven-year Tribulation period), the Antichrist will go into the temple in the city of Jerusalem and desecrate the temple by walking into the Holy of Holies and claiming to be God (2 Thessalonians 2:4).

## A Heavenly Battle

Also at the midway point of the Tribulation, there will be a battle in the heavenlies, according to Revelation 12:7-17, between the good angels, under the leadership of Michael the archangel, and Satan and all of his evil angels.

The Lord will direct Michael to take Satan and all of his evil angels and cast them out of heaven. The Bible speaks of three heavens: The first heaven is the heaven that we can see in the daytime—the sun and the clouds. The second heaven is the area where the stars and the galaxies are located, and the third heaven is the location where God is today.

Michael will take the evil angels and Satan and throw them out of the heavens onto the earth. Those in the heavens will rejoice and give praise for the fact that the devil has been thrown out. Revelation 12:12 says, "Therefore rejoice, ye heavens, and ye that dwell in them. Woe to the inhabiters of the earth and of the sea! For the devil is come down unto you, having great wrath, because he knoweth that he hath but a short time" (KJV).

## The Dragon and the Woman

Revelation 12:13 tells us that the dragon, defined in Scripture as Satan, will be cast upon the earth and he will persecute the woman who brought forth a male child. That's apocalyptic literature referring to the Jewish people today.

Revelation 12:13-17 reveals that when these evil angels and Satan are thrown upon the earth, they will do what they can to destroy the Jewish people. The entire Jewish world will come under fire.

Again, if Satan is able to destroy the Jewish people, then God will be unable to keep His promise to the Jewish people that they would be a nation. According to the Abrahamic covenant, they would have a land forever, the land covenant (Deuteronomy 30). There is also the promise that God gave to David, the Davidic covenant, 2 Samuel 7, that there would be a temple on the Temple Mount in the city of Jerusalem where a son of David would rule as King of kings and Lord of lords forever and ever.

Revelation 12:13,17 is the Scripture that reveals that Satan will do whatever he can to destroy all of the Jewish people in the last half of the Tribulation period, which is referred to as the Great Tribulation by Jesus Christ in Matthew 24. In fact it will be so bad at that time, Daniel 12:1 tells us that God will have to instruct Michael the archangel to come and protect the Jewish people before they are completely wiped off the face of the earth. This, as we have said in previous pages of this book, refers to Israel under fire in a terrible time in history.

In the last three-and-a-half years of the Tribulation period, in addition to Satan doing everything he can to destroy the Jewish people on the earth, Satan will have his representative the Antichrist become the leader of a one-world economic, political governmental system that will be headquartered in the literal city of Babylon.

Revelation 18 uses the name Babylon three times, uses the word city six times, and the word great eight times, referring to the great city of Babylon. The city of Babylon will be the headquarters for the Antichrist after the false prophet (Revelation 13:14-15) sets up an image of the Antichrist in the temple that has been desecrated at the midway point of the Tribulation period.

## The Mark of the Beast

During this last three-and-a-half years, the Antichrist will also put in place a global economic structure that will cause everyone who wants to buy or sell products, food, clothing, or pay for housing to sustain life, to receive an identification mark referred to as the "mark of the beast" in Revelation 13:16-17.

Those who do not have this mark will not be able to buy or sell. The merchants, according to Revelation 18, will join forces with the Antichrist and will become rich. Everyone on the face of the earth will come under the rule of the Antichrist, who will be ruling his economic, political, governmental system from his headquarters in the literal city of Babylon. Many have suggested that Babylon was destroyed in Daniel 5, but as you read in Ezra 7 (verses 6 and 9), you discover that the Jewish scribe Ezra, some 75 years after the fall of the Babylonian Empire in 539 B.C., was living in the city of Babylon before he took his journey to Jerusalem. In Ezra's day, Babylon was still a very viable city.

Two hundred years after the fall of the Babylonian Empire, Alexander the Great set up his headquarters for the Grecian Empire in the city of Babylon. And 1 Peter 5:13 refers to a church in the city of Babylon that was established by the apostle Peter, who was being obedient to Jesus Christ, who told him to go into the uttermost parts of the earth to give the gospel out. This was 500 years after the fall of the Babylonian Empire.

In Peter's day, the city of Babylon was the second most populated Jewish city in the world, second only to the city of Jerusalem. Babylon still exists today, and it is not a city that has been completely destroyed as called for in Isaiah 13-14, Jeremiah 50-51, and Revelation 16:17-21; 18:10,17,19. "Babylon," modern-day Iraq, is being rebuilt after the removal of Saddam Hussein, the treacherous dictator who ruled the people of Iraq for so many years.

With the economic crisis that our world is facing today, it seems like the perfect situation for the Antichrist to come to power and control the economies of the world. When world leaders at the G20 met together to try to solve the global economic crisis, the European Union called for the establishment of a global governance structure that would subject all financial market activities around the world to regulation and be backed by a system of inescapable sanctions against violators.[*] Could today's events be leading toward the global financial control and governance the Bible predicts will take place?

It is also during these last three-and-a-half years of the Tribulation period that God will prepare a place to protect the Jewish people (Revelation 12:6), a place where at least one-third of the Jews will be protected, their lives saved, and they will come to know Jesus as their Messiah. He will be their God, and they will be His people (Zechariah 13:9).

This location is the city of Petra according to what the Bible describes in Isaiah 63:1-6. It is interesting to note that when Israel signed a peace agreement with Jordan back in October of 1994, one of the articles in that peace agreement called for the exchange of tourists between the two countries, Israel and Jordan.

While serving as a journalist in the city of Jerusalem during that time, I (Jimmy) was not only able to cover that peace treaty signing, but did man-on-the-street interviews with Jewish people. I asked them what they thought was the most significant aspect of the peace treaty between Israel and Jordan. About 95 percent of those questioned said they would now be able to have the opportunity to visit Petra, a location that every Jewish person would love to be able to visit sometime

* Ted R. Bromund and J.D. Foster, "The G-20 Summit: Potential Threats to U.S. Interests," The Heritage Foundation. March 20, 2009. Accessed at http://www.heritage.org/research/europe/wm2352.cfm.

in their lifetime. God may be putting into the hearts of the Jewish people a desire to go to Petra, where He will protect them during the terrible time of Jacob's trouble, the last three-and-a-half years of the Tribulation period. At the end of the seven-year Tribulation period, Revelation 18:10,17,19 tell us that this city of Babylon, headquarters for the Antichrist and his one-world economic, political, governmental system, will be destroyed. In fact, it says it will be destroyed in one hour. This is a prophecy that must be fulfilled, according to not only Revelation 18, but the other passages of prophecy already mentioned, Isaiah 13–14 and Jeremiah 50–51. The prophecy pertaining to how this will take place is Revelation 16:17-21.

Before we look at the actual prophecy pertaining to the destruction of the literal city of Babylon, go back with me to Jeremiah 50 and 51. Remember that 2 Peter 1:20 tells us that "no prophecy of Scripture is a matter of one's own interpretation" (NASB). You cannot study through the book of Revelation—which quotes the Old Testament over 300 times—and its prophetic statements without understanding what the Old Testament prophets were talking about as well. These prophecies must fit like a hand in a glove as they come to a conclusion as to how this will all work out.

## The Destruction of Babylon

At the end of the seven-year Tribulation period, Babylon is going to be completely destroyed. Jeremiah 50–51 talks about the wrath of God in 50:13. Jeremiah wrote, "Because of the indignation of the Lord she will not be inhabited, but she will be completely desolate" (NASB). Jeremiah 50:40 states Babylon will be overthrown like Sodom and Gomorrah, and "No man will live there, nor will any son of man reside in it" (NASB).

Jeremiah 51:37,43 also describes the destruction of Babylon. It states God's wrath will fall on the city because of what King Nebuchadnezzar of the Babylonian Empire did to the Jewish temple on the Temple Mount in Jerusalem.

Jeremiah 50:28 says, "The voice of them that flee and escape from the land of Babylon, declares in Zion [Zion is synonymous with Jerusalem] the vengeance of the LORD our God, the vengeance of His temple" (NKJV).

You might remember Belshazzar on the night the Babylonian Empire fell. It was not the city of Babylon that fell. It was the Babylonian Empire that fell. According to Daniel 5:1-4, Belshazzar had called for the implements that his grandfather, Nebuchadnezzar, had brought out of the Jewish temple in Jerusalem and into the captivity.

Belshazzar used these implements (vessels sanctified for service in the Jewish temple in Jerusalem) during his drunken party with 1,000 of his nobles whom he had invited. On that night, the Medes and the Persians defeated the Babylonian Empire. But it is because of this event that the Lord will destroy the literal city of Babylon and fulfill all the prophecies that call for this to happen.

Current events in our day seem to be setting the stage for these Bible prophecies to be fulfilled. We should not allow current events to drive our understanding of Bible prophecy, but rather we should study the scenario that God has laid out in these prophetic passages describing end-time events. Understanding these passages will help us analyze current events to see if they are setting the stage for these prophecies to be fulfilled.

With all that is going on in the Middle East—with the alignment of nations and Iraq being the central focus of many political campaigns in recent years—these events should draw our attention to understand the scenario that God lays out in the book of Revelation. Revelation 16 describes the destruction of the city of Babylon, which is the seventh of the vial judgments. Let me remind you that there are twenty-one judgments in the book of Revelation. There are seven seal judgments, found in chapter 6 of Revelation with the seventh one in chapter 8:1. There will be seven trumpet judgments (Revelation chapters 8, 9, and 11). And then the seven vial or bowl judgments (Revelation 16). These judgments get progressively worse through the Tribulation period.

The last of the 21 judgments is found in Revelation 16:17. Finally the seventh angel poured out his vial into the air, and a loud voice came out of the temple from the throne saying it is done. Verse 18 speaks about a great earthquake, an earthquake like has never been felt upon the face of the earth. Verse 19 deals with the great city of Babylon being destroyed. Verses 20-21 talk about how even gigantic hailstones, weighing about a hundred pounds each, will be cast down upon the city of Babylon. This stronghold for the Antichrist, this one-world economic, political, governmental system headquartered in Babylon the last three-and-a half years of the Tribulation period, will be totally destroyed (Revelation 18:10, 17, 19) "in one hour." This will be the fulfillment of God's wrath upon the city of Babylon.

## The Battle of Armageddon

In the passages that we have been studying, we see that the Jewish people are the ones under fire during this seven-year Tribulation period. But once the city of Babylon is destroyed, the Bible changes our focus to the city of Jerusalem. At that point in time the Antichrist will gather all of the armies of the world there. Revelation 16:13-16 is a parenthetical passage and says that this Satanic trinity (Satan, the Antichrist, and the false prophet) will use signs, wonders, and miracles to gather all the armies of the world into the city of Jerusalem for the Battle of Armageddon.

The term *Battle of Armageddon* is probably not a good term to use. It should be referred to instead as the *Campaign of Armageddon*. The battle itself will take place in the Jezreel Valley in the center of the State of Israel. But the Campaign of Armageddon actually begins in the city of Jerusalem.

The ancient Jewish prophet Zechariah revealed what will happen in that day. In fact, he uses the phrase "day of the Lord" in Zechariah 14:1-2, saying, "I will gather all the nations to Jerusalem to fight against it."

There will be a number of Jews still living in the city of Jerusalem in addition to those who will be protected in Petra. Petra is located across the Jordan Valley to the south of the Dead Sea in the modern-day nation of Jordan, where it is one of the seven wonders of the world. As the armies of the world gather in Jerusalem and endeavor to destroy the city, the Lord Jesus Christ will leave the heavens and come back to the earth. Revelation 19:11 says, "I saw heaven opened" (NASB). John sees the Messiah, Jesus Christ, riding on a white horse, coming back to the earth. Verse 14 describes how the armies, which are in heaven, will follow Him upon white horses back to the earth.

Those armies are comprised of Christians who will have been taken to the heavenlies to be with Jesus Christ at the rapture of the church before the seven-year Tribulation period. When Jesus comes back, He comes back to the city of Jerusalem (Zechariah 14:4), plants His feet on the Mount of Olives, and the Mount of Olives will split in the middle before Jerusalem from east to west by a very large valley. That great valley will open up a way for these armies of the world, gathered in Jerusalem, to make their way up to the Jezreel Valley in Israel (some 97 miles away) to fight against Jesus Christ.

By the way, it has been suggested that if all of the nations of the world bring their armies to Jerusalem, there may be around 100 million soldiers gathered against Jesus Christ. They will join the forces of Satan, the Antichrist, and the false prophet to try to stop the true Messiah, Jesus Christ, from coming back and setting up His kingdom in the city of Jerusalem.

According to the book of Ezekiel, Jesus Christ will reconstruct the city of Jerusalem. Instead of eight-and-a-half square miles (as it is today), it will be 2,500 square miles. The Temple Mount will be enlarged from what it is today to be one square mile in size. It will also be raised up above the enlarged city of Jerusalem. According to Zechariah 6:12-13, on top of the Temple Mount, Jesus Christ will build a temple from which He will rule during the 1,000-year period of time known as the millennial kingdom, which follows the Battle of Armageddon.

As the armies of the world retreat to the Jezreel Valley to prepare for the battle that will take place there, Jesus Christ builds His temple in Jerusalem (Zechariah 6:12), and then He makes His way to the Jezreel Valley.

The Jezreel Valley is some 14 miles wide, 67 miles long, and approximately 1,000 square miles in dimension. So it would be very easy for 100 million soldiers to gather there. Jesus Christ will go up to the Jezreel Valley and defeat the world's armies—these Gentile world powers who have come against not only Him, but the Jewish people who will have been under fire for this seven-year Tribulation period.

Jesus Christ will defeat these armies and make His way over to Petra. You may ask, "How do we know He goes to Petra?" The prophet Isaiah had a vision. He saw someone traveling from Edom in the area of Bozrah (Isaiah 63:1-6). Matthew 24:15-16 records Jesus' prophetic statement:

> Therefore when you see the "abomination of desolation,"
> spoken of by Daniel the prophet, standing in the holy place
> (whoever reads, let him understand), then let those who
> are in Judea flee to the mountains (NKJV).

The Jewish people will heed this prophecy and flee to the mountainous wilderness in Southern Jordan (Edom) to a city called Bozrah. The ancient Roman city called Petra is that same city.

Isaiah 63:1 says Jesus Christ will be coming in the greatness of His strength, He that is righteous and mighty to save. Isaiah will ask the question in 63:2, "Why is your apparel red, and your garments like one who treads in the winepress?" (NKJV). This is what Revelation 14:19-20 refers to when it says the blood from the armies will flow as high as the horses' bridle for 176 miles from the Jezreel Valley, and all the way over to Petra.

## Jesus' Triumph Over the Satanic Trinity

Then Jesus will make His way across the Jordan Valley, up the back side of the Mount of Olives, across the Kidron Valley, through the Eastern

Gate and into the Temple Mount area to enter into the Holy of Holies (Ezekiel 43:1-7). Jesus walks into the Holy of Holies and sits down on the throne in fulfillment of the Davidic covenant, which was given to the Jewish people, to King David in 2 Samuel 7. The text says there will be a King of the Jewish people in the city of Jerusalem, seated in a Jewish temple in the Holy of Holies, and it will be one of the sons of King David. Jesus Christ qualifies in every aspect of this promise. The kingdom that God had promised the Jewish people will be set up.

Remember that at the rapture of the church, Christians will go into the presence of Jesus Christ. Revelation 19:7-9 talks about the marriage ceremony and the marriage supper of the Lamb. This is the marriage of Jesus Christ, the groom, to the bride, the church. This marriage takes place just before the Tribulation begins and the marriage supper of the Lamb will last the entire seven years of the Tribulation period.

The Judgment Seat of Christ is the time when the Christians will be outfitted with their wedding garments. Revelation 19:8 speaks of our wedding garments as the "righteous acts of saints." These righteous acts of Christians will become the "wedding garment" for what Jesus will see at the marriage ceremony.

At that point in time, after Jesus Christ has come back to the earth, He will deal with the adversaries of the Jewish people who endeavored to wipe them off the face of the earth during the Tribulation period. Then He will deal with the two members of the Satanic trinity: the Antichrist, which is the beast in Revelation 19:20, will be taken, and then along with him the false prophet, who performed false miracles which deceived people and led them to receive the mark of the beast, will be taken to judgment. They will both be cast alive into a lake of fire, burning with brimstone (Revelation 19:20).

Satan, who energized both the Antichrist and the false prophet, will be cast into the bottomless pit (Revelation 20:1-3) where he will be chained for this 1,000-year millennial kingdom period. At the end of it, he will be loosed for a short season, but then finally will be cast into the lake of fire. Revelation 20:4-6 describes the Tribulation saints, many of whom are the Jewish people who have trusted in Jesus Christ during that terrible time of judgment. Revelation 20:4 says, "And I saw thrones, and they sat on them, and judgment was committed to them. Then I saw the souls of those who had been beheaded for their witness to Jesus and for the word of God, who had not worshiped the beast or his image, and had not received his mark on their foreheads or on their hands. And they lived and reigned with Christ for a thousand years." These are Tribulation saints, which will include many Gentiles and a number of the Jewish people who had come under fire during the Tribulation.

Some of them were beheaded because of their witness for Jesus; none of them were willing to worship the beast nor take the mark of the beast while they lived. These will rule with Jesus Christ for the 1,000-year period of time.

Jewish believers will be the "hands-on" leaders in the kingdom period across the earth, and the kingdom will fulfill the promise God made to the Jewish people in Daniel 7:13-14 and many other prophetic passages.

Jesus Christ will go into the temple and sit there as King of kings and Lord of lords for the Jewish people. He will rule and reign and He will fulfill the promises in the parables found in Matthew, Mark, Luke and John that relate to what the Jewish believers coming out of the Tribulation period will be able to do as they go through the 1,000-year millennial kingdom.

In the kingdom period, those Jews who were under fire during the Tribulation period will be lifted up to serve in their kingdom. These will be Jews who faced the armies of the world gathered to annihilate every Jew on the face of the earth. These will be Jews that were under fire during the times when Satan and his evil angels tried to destroy them. These will be Jews who endured all seven years of the Tribulation, even through the end when the armies of the world came to Jerusalem to destroy them. Jesus Christ will protect His chosen people, the Jewish people, who were under fire for this seven-year period of time.

Everything that we have revealed to you in the first part of this book, including our interviews with Jewish Israeli leaders, seems to be indicating that we are quickly approaching the time when all these particular scriptures about the terrible Tribulation time will come true. The information we learned sets the stage for our presentation of the book of Revelation and the fact that the Jewish people are approaching a time when they will come under fire. But it also means we are quickly approaching the time when Jesus Christ, the Messiah for the Jewish people, will come back to help those Jews under fire enter into a relationship with Him, not only for the millennial kingdom, but for all eternity as well.

There is additional information given in Revelation chapters 21 and 22 that describes the new heavens, the new earth, and the New Jerusalem. But on the subject of Israel under fire, we have been able to bring to your attention all that the book of Revelation reveals will happen in the last days.

This concludes our effort to provide a simple overview of the book of Revelation. Now, there are some issues we did not address—issues that have been raised by many people over the years at prophecy conferences we have taught at. In the next chapter, we'll share the ten most-frequently-asked questions and their answers.

# Chapter 13

# THE MOST-ASKED QUESTIONS ABOUT THE BOOK OF REVELATION

M any people have questions about the book of Revelation and the future. We have selected ten of the more frequently asked questions and placed them here. I (John) asked Jimmy to answer these questions in a special televised interview. I asked the questions and Jimmy answered them. We've included this material below in a form as close as possible to the taped version.

1.  *What happens to children at the rapture?*

We do not know for sure. There's no text in God's Word that gives us a definite answer. Many parents and grandparents ask me that particular question in prophecy question-and-answer sessions. What I tell them is twofold: First, King David said concerning the death of his small child, "I will go to him, but he will not return to me" (2 Samuel 12:23). This seems to indicate that his little boy went into the heavens, and David would be able to go and be with him. So we possibly have the assurance that at the time of the rapture, even children in the wombs of their mothers, will be taken up.

Second, in Matthew 18 Jesus said, "I tell you the truth, unless you change and become like little children, you will never enter the kingdom of heaven" (verse 3). He loves the little children. He dispatches guardian angels to take care of them. Though we do not know what is going to happen to the little children who have not reached the age of accountability, Jesus makes it clear He loves them so much that He will protect them. So we do not have to worry about them.

2. *Will people who do not accept Christ before the rapture have the opportunity to do so during the Tribulation period?*

I do *not* believe that there will be a second chance in the Tribulation period for people who go through these three steps: First, they hear the gospel. Second, they understand the gospel. And third, they reject the gospel of their own free will. Second Thessalonians 2:8-12 says that God shall send them a strong delusion, that they might believe the lie of Satan—that is, they'll believe the Antichrist will tell them how to gain salvation. They will not have a second chance.

But all those who have not yet heard the gospel will be able to hear it preached by the two witnesses and the 144,000 male virgin Jews as they spread across the world. In this seven-year-period of time, they will preach to every single person on earth. The only ones who will not have an opportunity to receive Jesus Christ are those who, before the rapture, heard, understood, and rejected the gospel.

3. *Some people say that the rapture occurs at the middle of the Tribulation; others say it occurs toward the end of the Tribulation. Why is it that you believe the Bible teaches the rapture comes before the Tribulation and that Christians will not be involved in any part of the Tribulation? What's the scriptural evidence?*

Revelation 3:10 is part of the letter that was written to all of those in attendance in the church at Philadelphia. And here Jesus promised, "I will...keep you from the hour of trial"—the Tribulation period. He didn't say, "I will *take* you through it." He said, "I will...keep you *from* the hour of trial." That's one reason. Second, the word "church" appears 25 times in the book of Revelation. It's used 19 times prior to chapter 4, when the rapture takes place, and it's used six times after Revelation 19:11, when Christ returns to the earth. It's used zero times in the 16 chapters that describe in minute detail, the seven-year period of time called the Tribulation. Either God forgot to include the church in the Tribulation, or God simply doesn't see Christians or the church being on earth during the Tribulation.

And there's another reason we're not going to be there. The purpose for the Tribulation is threefold: it's to win Jewish people to Jesus Christ, to bring an end to Gentile world powers, and to destroy the satanic Trinity (Satan, the Antichrist, and false prophet). The rapture will take Christians out of that period of time. Jesus will protect us from the wrath to come. He will take us away before that time of wrath begins.

### 4. *What will happen to Christians when the rapture occurs?*

First Corinthians 15:51 says that "in a flash, in the twinkling of an eye," we will be changed and stand before Jesus Christ. And at that point, the judgment seat of Christ will take place (2 Corinthians 5:10). Romans 14:10 says that we will all give an account of ourselves before God. All Christians will stand at the judgment seat of Christ, but not to determine whether they are saved or lost. You'll only get to the judgment seat of Christ if you're saved. The judgment seat of Christ is for the purpose of judging our works for Christ—whether they were good or no good. The good works are referred to as gold, silver, and precious stones in 1 Corinthians 3. They are the works we have done in His power for His glory. In that same passage in 1 Corinthians 3, there are works that are referred to as wood, hay, and stubble. Those are the works Christians will have done in their own power and for their own selfish glory. Those works will be burned up; and those believers will suffer loss of rewards.

At the judgment seat of Christ, a Christian may receive anywhere from one to as many as five crowns. First Corinthians 9:27 talks about a crown incorruptible, for bringing your body under subjection. First Thessalonians 2:19 talks about a crown of rejoicing, for being a soulwinner.

James 1:12 talks about a crown of life that is given to those who yield not to temptation. Now, temptation itself is not sin. It's *yielding* to temptation that becomes the sin. Don't yield to temptation, and you will get a crown of life. First Peter 5:1-4 talks about a crown of glory for those Christians who help other members of the body of Christ to grow. The apostle Paul said, "I have finished the race, I kept the faith. Now there is in store for me the crown of righteousness...and not only to me, but also to all who have longed for his appearing" (2 Timothy 4:7-8). According to Revelation 4:10, all those crowns will be taken by believers to the throne where Jesus is seated and laid at His feet in thanksgiving.

Our good works will also result in us being given wedding garments to wear. We will be married to Jesus Christ. After the judgment seat of Christ, there will be a marriage ceremony. Revelation 19:7-9 talks about the marriage ceremony and about our garments, which will depend on our righteous acts, which, in turn, will be determined at the judgment seat of Christ.

And then, of course, Revelation 19:9 talks about the time of joy and celebration at the marriage supper of the Lamb. Now a Jewish wedding ceremony lasts for seven days, but our ceremony in heaven will last for seven years. After those seven years we will then ride upon white horses (see Revelation 19:11-14) and return to the earth with Jesus Christ. The marriage supper of the Lamb and the celebration will happen in the heavenlies while damnation and judgment are taking place on the earth.

5. *How does Jesus' teaching about the rapture in John 14 parallel the events of a Jewish wedding?*

In John 14, Jesus said, "Do not let your hearts be troubled." I am sure His disciples were having anxiety attacks in the upper room. He had told them that He was going to be crucified. He said not to worry about it. "Do not let your hearts be troubled. Trust in God; trust also in me. In my Father's house are many rooms; If it were not so, I would have told you. I am going there to prepare a place for you. And if I go...I will come back and take you to be with me that you also may be where I am."

Jesus has returned back to His Father's house to prepare the place He talked about for us. In a Jewish wedding, the bride-to-be and the groom-to-be come together with their respective fathers. The fathers say, "Okay, we agree to the marriage." And then the groom-to-be says to his bride-to-be, "Honey, my dad said I can add an apartment to our family home. That is where we will live. I am going to add to my father's house; I am going to prepare a place for us. You go prepare your wedding garments. And when I am finished, I will come and get you."

In New Testament Jewish culture, the father made the decision regarding when the apartment is ready. He would then say to his son, "Son, the apartment is ready. Go get your bride." Immediately, the son would call his best man. And I've seen this happen in the Old City of Jerusalem in the orthodox quarter there. The best man will walk though the streets shouting, "Behold, the bridegroom cometh!" They would then go over to the bride's house, and there the marriage ceremony would then take place. After that, they consummate the marriage with sexual union. The groom then steps out and says, "The marriage has been consummated. Let the party begin." And for seven days, everyone at the wedding celebrates.

Remember when Jesus went to the wedding at Cana of Galilee? John 2, says He arrived on the *third day*. I've been to one of those seven-day wedding feasts and celebrations. I got there on the fifth day. Unbelievably, they were still having a party to celebrate this new marriage!

As we await the rapture, we're in the engagement period with Jesus Christ. He has returned to His Father's house. Remember His answer to the disciples when they asked, "When are You coming back?" He said, "Only My Father knows. He will tell Me when to go get My bride." When that happens, the rapture will take place. The parallel between a Jewish wedding and what Jesus will do with us (His bride) is beautiful.

6. *After Jesus Christ returns to earth, after the Tribulation events are over, where will Christians reside? Will Christians stay on the earth? Will they go back and forth between heaven and earth? What happens to Christians during the millennial kingdom?*

We will be married to Jesus Christ, King of kings and Lord of lords. Now, let's think logically for a moment. If you're the bride to the king, what does that make you? It makes you the queen. So, we will reign with Christ during the millennial kingdom. We will be with Jesus Christ. First Thessalonians 4:17 says that from the time of the rapture onward, we will never leave His presence. As His bride, we will rule with Him. The pattern for the kingdom was set up in Genesis 1:26 when God let Adam and Eve have dominion. That dominion is reigning—it's a kingdom. And this first kingdom was set up there in the Garden of Eden. It was because of sin that Adam and Eve did not continue on. And so Jesus Christ and His bride—as husband and wife—will rule in Jerusalem for a thousand years. We will be with Christ and reign with Him.

7. *Where is the United States of America in Bible prophecy?*

John, that is the most-asked question in my Bible prophecy question-and-answer sessions. The United States is not mentioned anywhere in prophecy. In Zechariah 14:2, we read that all the nations of the world will gather at Jerusalem at the end of the Tribulation before Christ comes back. If America is still on this earth after the rapture and during the Tribulation, it will gather with the other nations at Jerusalem.

Here is another way to look at it: I believe at the rapture of the church, the millions of Christians who are the backbone of this nation will be taken up to heaven. And a nation on the slippery slope to moral, educational, military, and economic decay will be judged by God. I believe America will fall from its pedestal of power and that it will have little influence by the end of the Tribulation. This is just one possibility of what could happen to America during the Tribulation.

8. *People want to know about the Antichrist. Some people claim that he is going to be Jewish. Do you think the Antichrist will be Jewish?*

No. The Antichrist will be a Gentile empowered by Satan. Daniel 7:7 mentions the ten horns that represent the fourth Gentile world power. Verse 24 reveals this will be the revived Roman Empire. Out of those ten horns will come a little horn. That's one of 27 names for the Antichrist. So, he comes out of the Gentile world. Revelation 13, which is the most detailed passage of Scripture on the Antichrist, talks about and refers back to Daniel 7; it talks about a connection with a leopard, a bear, and a lion. Those same images were in the vision Daniel had in Daniel 7. Again, that's talking about the Gentile world. The Antichrist will be a Gentile.

But why will the Jews accept him as their Messiah? Second Thessalonians 2:11, says that anyone who refuses to listen to the truth will receive a "powerful delusion so that they believe the lie." Any Jew during this seven-year period of time who trusts in Jesus Christ will certainly not accept the Antichrist as the Messiah, but they *will* believe in Jesus, the true Messiah. But every Jew or Gentile who rejects Jesus Christ during that period of time, will receive a strong delusion from God so that they will believe the lie.

9. *Recently the Oak Ridge National Laboratory received a new computer that is 55,000 times faster than your typical PC. It can do more than one quadrillion mathematical calculations per second. This would be equivalent to having every person in the world perform one mathematical calculation every second for 650 years. That is what this computer can do in one single day.*

*People want to know about modern technology and its possible connections to the mark of the beast. Should people be concerned that using today's technology could somehow set them up for having the mark of the beast?*

Let's go back to the mark of the beast in the Bible. Revelation 13:15-17 says that during the Tribulation, people will be forced to receive the mark of the beast, which will be on their forehead or the back of their hand. And that mark will be required if they want to buy or sell. They cannot do that unless they have received the mark of the beast.

Revelation 13:18 says the number of the beast is 666. We tend to equate the mark with the number, but there is no absolute proof that 666 will be used on the forehead or the back of the hand. We're not told what the mark will be or what it will look like. We cannot assume anything that the Bible does not state clearly.

I don't know exactly what the mark will be. The Bible is silent about that. All non-Christians in the Tribulation period will understand and have the mark of the beast. And those who know Christ as Lord and Savior won't have to worry about the mark of the beast. So if you get a computer chip for your job so you can clock in and out of work, don't be worried about that. That's not the mark of the beast because the Antichrist is not yet on the scene. Is that the kind of technology they might use? It may well be. The computers being developed may also already be able to handle the calculations needed to process the marks. But if you know Jesus Christ as Lord and Savior, you'll never have to be concerned about the mark of the beast. You'll be gone at the rapture of the church. The mark will be given only to those who reject Jesus Christ.

## 10. What's the difference between Hades now and Gehenna later?

In the Bible, Hades is a location referred to as Abraham's bosom or Paradise. When Jesus was hanging on the cross, He told the thief who believed in Him, "Today, you will be with me in *paradise*" (Luke 23:43). Paradise is a location, and we get the information about it from Luke 16, where it is called "Abraham's bosom" (verse 22 NASB). I don't think the story in Luke 16 was a parable. I believe that Lazarus and the rich man were both real men who died. The rich man immediately went into torment in Hades, a holding area for the dead at that time before the resurrection of Christ. And Lazarus immediately was carried by the angels into the place called Abraham's bosom. Those are the places the rich man and Lazarus went to, and there was a great gulf fixed between them.

I believe Ephesians 4 teaches that Jesus, after His death and burial, descended into Hades. He preached, and then He took captivity captive. He took all of those who were in Paradise into the heavenlies, where all those who die in Christ will go at their death. Those who were in torment will remain in Hades until the Great White Throne Judgment, which is the third event, or the third pillar, of our three main events in the book of Revelation. The text in Revelation 20:11-15, says death and Hades will be delivered up to Jesus Christ at the Great White Throne Judgment. That is, He will sentence the occupants of Hades at that time. They will all be unbelievers and they will go into the lake of fire because their names are not written in the Book of Life. And they will be in the lake of fire forever with Satan, the Antichrist, and the false prophet.

In Matthew 24, Jesus Christ was asked to talk about the signs of His second coming. When He responded to His disciples, He did not talk about the rapture of the church. That was not on His mind at that time. He talked about the second coming; He talked about the Tribulation events described in the book of Revelation. He talked about deceptions in the form of sign, wonders, and miracles (Matthew 24:4,5,11,24). We see a proliferation of such things today, and Jesus said they would be the first signs of how the world will be before He returns.

Then Jesus talked about wars and rumors of wars—nation against nation, kingdom against kingdom, and people against people. He said that would happen before He comes back. It is so evident in our world that today we have wars and rumors of wars. Just look at the Middle East conflict—Fatah and Hamas (the two factions of the Palestinians)—are killing each other. I believe there will be a civil war in Israel—Jew against Jew—because there are Jews living in Judea and Samaria whom the Israeli government wants to evacuate from their land. But they say

"You can't remove us." You look at Afghanistan, Iraq, and Iran, and you can see wars and rumors of wars going on in our world.

Then Jesus said there would be famine. People will starve to death. He said there will be earthquakes in diverse places. Basically, Matthew 24 is a preview of the book of Revelation. And what I have just given you is a list of events that corresponds to the sealed judgments in Revelation 6 that happen after the rapture of the church. Jesus finished the Olivet Discourse with Matthew 24:32-34, telling His disciples to learn the parable of the fig tree. That has nothing to do with the State of Israel. He was on the Mount of Olives, and a fig tree was right beside Him. It was in the springtime, and tree leaves were starting to pop up all around. We can imagine Him saying, "You see the leaves on that limb there? That indicates summer is almost here. So likewise when you see all of these things, know that it is near." What's near?

When the disciples asked Jesus when He would return, they were not asking about the rapture, but the second coming—when He comes back to earth to rule. He said, "I tell you the truth, this generation will certainly not pass away until these things have happened" (verse 34). Who is He talking about? Not the people present with Him that day on the Mount of Olives. Rather, He was talking to a generation of people alive during the Tribulation. That is the generation of people who will see these things happen. When they see these things, they will know His second coming is close.

But again, the rapture must occur before the Tribulation, and we as Christians today are standing outside of the Tribulation period, before the rapture of the church. And we are seeing some of those signs of the last days beginning to happen. If we can see the stage being set for the Tribulation events to happen, I would suggest that we're living in the generation that will see the rapture of the church. And from the heavenlies, we will see the Tribulation unfold. Then we will return back to the earth with Jesus Christ.

# A FINAL WORD[13]

*"If there ever was an hour when men should consider their personal relationship to Jesus Christ, it is today."*

—Dr. John Walvoord[14]

In the midst of the uncertainties in our world today, the God who rules over history makes some promises that offer a hope and future. God wants to have a personal relationship with you *now*. He wants to free you from the guilt and issues in your life *now*, no matter who you are or what you have done.

As we approach the end of our journey together, would you allow us the opportunity to ask seven vital questions regarding your personal future? We hope and pray that your answers will help you prepare for life in this world and the next.

As people lie in bed at night and reflect back on the activities of the day, many probing questions often surface. These sometimes include even the deepest of spiritual questions, such as, "How good do you have to be to enter heaven? What do I really believe about God?" As we take time to consider these questions, we hope you will find our thoughts helpful.

*1. How good do you have to be to get into heaven?*

I (John) recently saw a survey that found that a majority of people still believe there is a hell, but less than one percent believe they will go there. Most people think they are just as good as anyone else, or maybe even better. But what if the average "good person" doesn't make it?

So how good *does* a person have to be to get into heaven? According to Jesus, you must be perfect, or you won't get in. In Matthew's Gospel, Jesus told His listeners, "I tell you, that unless your righteousness surpasses that of the Pharisees and the teachers of the law, *you will certainly not enter the kingdom of heaven*" (Matthew 5:20). At that time the Pharisees tried to keep more than five hundred laws every day to please God. Even though the religious leaders didn't always accomplish their goal, the average person thought they were doing well to live as righteously as the teachers of the law. They were shocked when Jesus said you have to go *beyond* the level of the Pharisees to make it.

A little later, Jesus clarified this even further. He said, "Be perfect, therefore, even as your heavenly Father is perfect" (Matthew 5:48). In other words, if you're not as perfect as God, don't even *think* you'll make it into heaven.

How does this apply to us now? Do you think God will let *you* into heaven? Because none of us could never be good enough to stand before God, Jesus provides eternity as a free gift. He said, "God did not send His Son into the world to condemn the world, but to save the world through him" (John 3:17). Peter wrote, "Christ died for sins once for all, the righteous for the unrighteous, to bring you to God" (1 Peter 3:18).

*2. Would you like Jesus to connect you with God?*

The apostle Paul said that God "made Him [Jesus] who knew no sin to be sin on our behalf, that we might become the righteousness of God in Him" (2 Corinthians 5:21 NASB). This means that when Jesus was crucified on the cross, God picked up our sins along with the sins of the entire world and placed them upon Jesus. Jesus became guilty of all of our sins in a legal sense. Paul was quick to point out that Jesus had no sins of His own, but that He became our substitute. Jesus died so we could have eternal life (John 11:25-26; Romans 6:23).

Paul wrote that God offers this new life through Christ as a free gift when you place your faith in Him. "This righteousness from God comes through *faith* in Jesus Christ to all who believe—there is no difference—they are justified freely *by His grace*" (Romans 3:22). So whether you have struggled with extremely difficult life choices or you consider yourself just an everyday person who has made mistakes, God is willing to provide the perfect righteousness you need to stand before Him.

I (John) taped a television program with a young man who had placed his trust in Christ after having been a homosexual prostitute. A month after we taped that program, this man died from AIDS. My friend Dr. Erwin Lutzer also knew this man. One day when we were taping a broadcast together, Erwin referred to this person, saying, "Think of two books. The first is called *The Life and Times of Roger* (not his real name). A second book is called *The Life and Times of Jesus Christ*. When you open the covers of *The Life and Times of Roger*, you see all the sins of Roger's life. There for everyone to witness are lust and broken relationships. Roger had over 1,100 sexual partners during his life, leaving a trail of lies, anger, and hurt toward many of the lives around him. Yet if you open the cover of the second book, *The Life and Times of Jesus Christ*, you'll see it contains all of Christ's perfections and absolute purity.

"Now picture what happened the moment Roger placed his faith in Christ. God ripped off the covers of both books and got rid of the contents of *The Life and Times of Roger*. He then placed between the covers of Roger's book the contents of *The Life and Times of Jesus Christ*. After that, every time God opens *The Life and Times of Roger*, he sees only the perfect life of Christ. This is what justification by faith truly means."

3. *How much faith do I need to get into heaven?*

The Bible says, "Believe on the Lord Jesus Christ, and you will be saved" (Acts 16:31 NKJV). Believing on Jesus is not just accepting facts about Jesus, though these facts are the foundation for faith. Just believing that Christ lived, died on the cross, and rose from the dead is not true faith. True faith is when you transfer all of your *trust* to Jesus.

One day a famous tightrope walker strung a wire across Niagara Falls. In front of a crowd of people, he jumped up on the wire and walked from the Canadian side to the American side and back again. Many people gathered to watch him. Then he put a wheelbarrow on the wire and filled it with sandbags weighing over 200 pounds. He successfully took that wheelbarrow with the sandbags across the falls and back. Next, he paused and asked the people who were gathered, "How many of you think I could place a *person* in this wheelbarrow and take him across the falls? Raise your hand." They all raised their hands, saying, "We believe you can do it." He then asked, "Who will be the first to get in?" No one would trust him with *their* life.

Jesus asks us, "Do you believe I am the Son of God who died for your sins, the one who can forgive you and offer you eternal life?"

You respond, "Lord, I believe."

Then Jesus says, "Then get into My wheelbarrow. Entrust your eternal destiny into My hands alone." If you will, Jesus promises that He will save you, enter your life, and enable you to live with power over sin. He will also give you eternal life. If you have not entrusted yourself into Jesus' hands, placing your faith solely in Him, why not now? The Bible promises, "Whoever will call upon the name of the Lord will be saved" (Romans 10:13 NASB). That "whoever" includes *you* the moment you place your faith in Christ alone.

4. *How much faith do you need?*

Beginning a relationship with Christ doesn't require a lot of faith. What is important is that you have faith, and that your faith has the proper focus.

Imagine that you're standing in an apartment building, two stories up. All of the exits are closed, you cannot leave the building, and it's starting to burn. Firemen arrive, carrying a rescue net. One of the firefighters looks up at you and shouts, "Jump!"

You look down and shout back, "No way!"

The fireman replies, "What choice do you have? If you stay there, you'll die."

"But I don't have enough faith."

"You don't have to have a *lot* of faith. Just step off of the building. We'll catch you."

In terms of Christ saving us, He doesn't require a lot of faith—just enough to step out and place ourselves in His hands. It's Jesus who does the saving, just like it's the firemen who help people in need of rescue. Whether your faith is big or small is not the issue—it is Jesus who does the saving.

But what if after you had jumped you discovered the firemen were not holding a net? Would you still be rescued? No! You would be in a desperate situation because you had faith in the wrong object. While true faith includes stepping out into the unknown, it also requires that you place that faith in a known reality, Jesus Christ.

*5. How do I begin a relationship with God?*

God knows our hearts and is not as concerned about our words as He is about our attitude. The following is a suggested prayer; you can pray your own prayer if you wish. It's not the prayer itself that saves you; it is trusting in Christ that saves you.

> *Dear Lord Jesus, I admit that I have sinned. I know I cannot save myself. Thank You for dying on the cross. I believe that Your death was for me and I receive Your sacrifice on my behalf. As best I can, I now transfer all of my trust from myself and anything that I would do to You. I open the door of my life to You*

*and by faith receive You as my Savior and Lord. Thank You
for forgiving my sins and giving me eternal life. Amen.*

## 6. *How do you* know *that Christ is in your life?*

"Here I am! I stand at the door and knock. If anyone hears my
voice and opens the door, I will come in and eat with him, and he
with me" (Revelation 3:20). Christ said that if anyone invites Him
into their life, He will enter that life.

The apostle John wrote, "These things I have written to you who
believe in the name of the Son of God, so that you may know that
you have eternal life" (1 John 5:13 NASB). If you have entrusted yourself
to Christ and have believed in Him, Scripture says God wants you to
know—not guess—that you have eternal life.

In Romans 10:13, the apostle Paul taught, "Whoever will call on
the name of the Lord will be saved" (NASB). He promises to save when
you call and trust in Christ. "But as many as received Him, to them
gave He the right to become children of God, to those who believe in
His name" (John 1:12 NKJV).

## 7. *Now what?*

Begin by sharing your decision with someone you know. Tell him
or her about the change that has taken place in your life. Then follow
through on your decision by learning more about Jesus Christ. This
includes reading God's Word, finding a Bible-teaching church, spending
time with other followers of Christ, and serving others from the
overflow of your transformed life.

Finally, please let us know about your choice to follow Jesus. We
would love to know about your spiritual commitment. Please contact
us with your story at stories@johnankerberg.org or write us at:

The Ankerberg Theological Research Institute
P.O. Box 8977
Chattanooga, TN 37414 USA

For more information about
John Ankerberg, see
www.johnankerberg.org

or call *The John Ankerberg Show* at
1-800-805-3030.


For more information about
Jimmy DeYoung, see
www.prophecytoday.com

or call Prophecy Today at
1-877-674-3298.

# INTERVIEW TRANSCRIPTS
# FEATURING BENJAMIN NETANYAHU

The following is from an exclusive interview with Benjamin Netanyahu that included a select group of journalists at a hearing inside
Jerusalem regarding the threat to Israel from Iran. This transcription is
provided by the Ankerberg Theological Research Institute and Shofar
Communications for information purposes only.

Mr. Benjamin Netanyahu is chairman of the Likud Party and Israel's thirteenth prime minister. He also served as the prime minister of
Israel between May 1996 and May 1999, elected in the first-ever direct
prime ministerial ballot. He served as the foreign minister in Prime
Minister Ariel Sharon's 2003 government, in which position he is cred-
ited with revolutionizing Israel's economy.

Mr. Netanyahu's diplomatic postings included serving as Israel's
ambassador to the United Nations, where he led the efforts to open
the U.N. Nazi war crimes archives in 1987. A former officer of Special
Forces and an MIT graduate, he is the author and editor of several
books.

Shared here are statements from this interview on issues related to
*Israel Under Fire,* some of which are not included in other portions
of this book.

## The Rise of Militant Islam in the World

"There is an opposing force that has been simmering for centuries and has been unleashed (first in the late 70s and late 1979 in Iran and then a decade later in Afghanistan) and these are the latent forces of militant Islam. [They are] latent because they have been brewing for centuries under the surface with an animus towards the very freedoms that I described. [They're trying] to regiment society according to… Islam. Obviously, there are two strains in this dogma—the militant Sunnis and the militant Shiites…The victory of the Mujahedin heralded the rise of al Qaeda.

"If you look at what has happened politically—not economically—to the world…you see a clear projectory of the rise of militant Islam. You see it not only taking over countries (which it has) but also extending its sway over many people…Obviously they haven't been able to take over the majority, and even the minority is small. But the minority of a very, very large majority is troubling in itself. But, their goals are unlimited. Whatever their successes so far, they don't intend to stop. They continue. Each of these militant strains [have been competing with each other]—who will produce the greater creed?"

## The Militant Shiites in Iran
## Are Racing to Destroy Israel

"The militant Sunnis bombed New York…Washington…and other targets, [such as] Bali [and] the European capitals. The militant Shiites in Iran are openly racing…to develop nuclear weapons with the explicit announced goal of wiping Israel from the face of the earth [and] re-establishing the caliphate (of course, under militant Shiite Iranian rule). The caliphate includes the territories from Iran to Spain. [They want to develop] long-range ballistic missiles first [targeting] every European capital, and within a decade [they want] to reach the eastern coast of the American mainland."

## Hezbollah Has Forty Thousand Rockets Aimed at Israel

"It used to be said Hezbollah [based in Lebanon] is a state within a state. It's not clear that has not been reversed, given that Hezbollah has now some forty thousand rockets, which is a lot more than they had before the second Lebanon war...They're much more lethal rockets—long-range rockets that can reach a good portion of this country. And this is all done by Iran. It cannot be understood as anything but an Iranian operation. And equally...they've already taken over half of Palestinian society...and they're agitating to take more."

## The Threat to the Oil Reserves in the Gulf

"Obviously, if Iran acquires nuclear weapons, everything that we've been talking about will pale in comparison...The power to extend [control, threaten, and] make good on the threats will be on a level that we have not seen, nor [is it] one that we can readily imagine. It will put the oil reserves of the gulf under their sway. They could easily bring down governments or fold them into their realm. They will inspire and encourage the radicals in the various Islamic communities that they're targeting around the world, and they will be in turn inspired by the fact that, obviously, the acquisition of nuclear weapons is a providential sign of the coming victory of the true believers. And, of course, they might make good on their twisted ideas of ending Zionism and extending their realm by other means. So this is [a] threat to the entire world, and it cannot be seen as anything but that."

## Iran Is Like Nazi Germany and Pushing to Obtain Nuclear Weapons

"I said a year-and-a-half ago that the year is 1938, and Iran is Germany. And it's racing to acquire nuclear weapons. Well, if that's the case, then we're in 1939. Our intelligence chiefs…publicly said it would take Iran three years to develop the critical knowledge to produce a weapon. Well, there are now about two years left; they haven't changed…their assessment [as far as I know.]

"So this a problem that we all face…It is hard sometimes in the daily flow of events to understand that something truly of historic proportions is taking place. I think there are two momentous processes [happening] before our eyes that [in retrospect] will be seen to have [greatly transformed] humanity, and they're competing with each other. They are like two rogue elephants charging right at each other. [All the freedom] of choice that one side represents [is] rejected by the other side—and violently rejected."

## What Can Be Done to Stop Iran from Obtaining Nuclear Weapons?

"The question is, what do we have to do? Well, it seems to me that the first thing we [as the very large civilized community of nations] have to do [is] everything in our power to prevent the arming of Iran with nuclear weapons. On this, I have to say, there is absolute unanimity in Israel. There is no opposition [or] coalition—not only on the declaratory level but on every other level. There are no party lines on this and there are no party divisions on this…I think this is a growing consensus. It wasn't always the case. The clarity of this threat wasn't always understood, but it is understood now, and we have absolute unanimity on this. And, I can say that in some of the leading governments in the world right now, there is [an equally] growing consensus. It may not extend as much to the public because the public is not aware of the full dimensions of this problem…

"The world will change for the worse if we don't stop [this problem] and all the other dimensions I spoke about. But how is this stopped? It can be stopped if sufficient pressure is brought about on the Iranian regime. And as was mentioned, I did pass (last week) a bill in our Knesset which I think is the toughest divestment bill. We took from all the divestment bills that we've seen in the United States...and also things that were done by the security council. And we amended them...and went beyond that to make it a criminal offense for a fund manager or a...financial institution...to knowingly invest in a company that is developing Iran's energy sector or its nuclear sector. And we allowed for other sectors, as well—there's a provision in the bill.

"We did this because we have been asking—and I've been doing this for quite some time—other governments and states within the United States to adopt these bills. And I'm happy to say that right now, I think it's about eight or nine or ten states (and some of them very big states) that are doing this, and this is a very big effort. And, I wanted to make sure that we practice what we preach...I have to say that again this was uniformly passed—opposition and coalition together—we joined on this. And this is the first thing that can be done. It's the enhancement of economic sanctions that fall basically into two categories: One category is the curtailing of banking activity, which is led by the United States government. And the second is the curtailment of investments in Iran's key sectors. The energy sector, by the way, provides the regime with eighty percent of its revenue. And this is one thing that should be done. There are political sanctions that could be put into place, like the movement of key personnel [who are] involved in these weapons programs and others.

"And there [are], of course, the other options which the American government has said should always be left open. I would say that, paradoxically, the nonmilitary options have much more weight and more clout if all options are left on the table...This is the minimum thing, and I believe that we could talk about many things. But I think...central [to] our policy [is the fact] that Iran must not acquire nuclear weapons. I think this is important, and it's important for all of us."

## If We Do Not Act, Time Is Not on Our Side

"The second point…is the question of how to stop the expansion of Iranian bases. And on this we do differ. But my purpose here was to try to draw attention to the fact that if we do not act, time is not on our side. It's on the other side. And that this is something that can be stopped if we harness sufficient will and courage and clarity towards this task. And that very much depends on an informed public opinion because most of the terror that we see today—indeed the thrust of the terror that we see today that you cover in your reporting—is basically Iranian-backed-and-inspired terror. The rockets…are basically thrust by indirect and sometimes…direct Iranian efforts. And that if Iran was blocked in this effort, then the chance for advancing peace would move—in my opinion—a lot faster."

## We Don't Seek a War with Anyone; We Seek Peace, But…

"We don't seek a war with anyone; we seek peace with all our neighbors, and that includes Syria, Iran, and so on—everyone, [and] certainly with our Palestinian neighbors. And this is what we'd like to do. When we speak about the security problems, we speak about the fact that we're being attacked [and] threatened. We are not only being told that we'll be wiped off the face of the earth, but also that Iranian-backed proxies are establishing themselves at our doorsteps and rocketing our people.

"Now…I don't know how many of you were here…during the second Lebanon War a year and a half ago. It's interesting to…hear what Hezbollah and Hamas were saying. Especially Hezbollah, [which] was rocketing northern Israel. They were rocketing the Galilee. They were rocketing Tiberias. They were rocketing Haifa. They were rocketing Acre…. And…you ask them, 'Why are you rocketing them?' And they say, 'Well, because we're rocketing occupied Palestine. Namely, we're rocketing occupied Haifa [and] occupied Tiberias.' And from the south...Hamas [was] rocketing occupied Ashkelon. And we might say, 'Wait a minute—we thought you limited your attacks merely to the West Bank, which is Judea-Samaria, disputed territory?' No. The occupation, they said, was any part of Israel, including—and...especially the pre-1967 part. This is deterrent—deliberately trying to rocket civilians."

## How Can You Negotiate with Someone Who Wants Your Destruction?

"The core of the problem that we face—the reason we don't have peace, in my opinion—is not today a territorial issue, but an existential issue. I think, in many ways, Middle Eastern politics have been overtaken. Nationalist sentiment has been overtaken by militant Islam, and militant Islam rejects any territorial or political solution. It wants the dissolution of the State of Israel. And this is the problem. This [is] the source of the problem. This is why it's becoming so dangerous. Because how can you negotiate with someone who wants your destruction? What will you negotiate—the terms of your disappearance?"

## Most Arab Governments Fear They Will Be Overtaken by Militant Islam

"This is the kind of thing that we're facing, so I want to make it clear that we're talking about how to defend ourselves—not how to initiate a conflict. And in so doing, I want to say...I don't think...we're alone. I think in most Arab governments today (and I'm weighing my words carefully by saying 'most') there is a fear that they, too, will be overtaken by the rising power of militant Islam. And, of course...arming... Iran with nuclear weapons would tremendously increase that power and thereby threaten not merely Israel but every Arab regime in the Middle East—more moderate and less moderate...everyone. This is not something that today we have to say to our Arab neighbors. I think to the Arab governments around us…whether or not they admit it publicly, this is what they think. Believe me, this is what they think."

## Hezbollah and Hamas
## Increase Their Attacks on Israel

"The second question is how to stop Iranian bases around us. Well, the first thing is, don't build any more of them. And if we have a disagreement today with the government, it is that the promise of additional Israeli withdrawals today means that the IDF [Israeli Defense Forces] walks out, and Hamas walks in. And if Hamas walks in, Iran walks in. Essentially this is what has happened, but not by design. I don't think this was the purpose [when] the Barak…government unilaterally and hastily left Lebanon in 2000, or of Sharon's government when it left Gaza.…. But the result has been the same—a tremendous increase in the power of Iran's proxies…of Hezbollah and…Hamas. So we have Hezbollah now with a tremendous base, and you can see that the international guarantees that were supposed to stop the flow of arms did nothing of the kind. So, we not only had four thousand rockets fired on the Galilee from that base, but we now have forty thousand rockets which are aimed at every part of Israel.

"And at the same time, the same thing has happened in the south. We've had, by the way, a tremendous increase in the power of Hamas. It…wasn't only politically strengthened, but very shortly afterward, it militarily just took over the Gaza Strip and kicked out the Palestinian Authority. And it's developed a base. They've rocketed four thousand rockets. That's the number since the unilateral disengagement…By the way, the rate is about…sixteen times—eighteen times? I don't remember what it was. [I mention it] just to give you a feeling of what we're talking about: a tremendous increase in the rate of rockets, maybe ten times. I'm not sure, but it's on that order of magnitude. And, of course, it's arming itself also. So we've got two bases that were created as a result of not having a partner there, and not having some security arrangements. We withdrew, they came in, and the rest is recent history.

"Now the question is, what do you do? And my point is...don't repeat the mistake the third time. Because, if we walk out here, there'll be an Iranian base here. Right here, across this street, on the other side of the street. That's what will happen.

"Now, we can stick to political correctness and pretend that's *not* going to be the case, but it *is* going to be the case. And, the reason that is the case is because of the endemic weakness in the Palestinian society...not only in [their] leadership. We always think it's leadership. It's not only leadership. It's that society itself is not strong enough to resist the onslaught of Hamas and [militant Islam.] So, what do you do about that? Well, theoretically, you have two options: One is you repeat the mistake, close your eyes, and hope for the best. And it's not going to happen. And, that's not something we recommend, to put it mildly. The second option is to do nothing, and I think that also has its costs, and I don't recommend that either.

"But, what our program is (and I'm glad to see that at least pieces of it are being adopted—in fact...the American government and others are trying to do something about it...) is to create stability and progress in Palestinian society [so we can] deprive the recruiting ground for the militant [Muslims] and to create, as I call it, 'bottom-up hope.' And how do you do that? Well...first...you've [got] to maintain security because if security collapses, everything goes down with it too. So, we recommend that we maintain security because...if we leave, it's not that Abbas will protect us. By staying, we protect ourselves, and we protect Abbas...and the Palestinian Authority [too.] Our goal is to protect ourselves, but this is a by-product.

"And...second...we develop a series of economic projects and define zones, and [we] push them forward rapidly. They have to be—among other things—not only infrastructure [and] money...but actually projects that are market-based [and] actually have a business logic to them.

And I think that we know how to do that. And if we form the government (and there's a good chance that we'll form the government), I intend to work with the Palestinian Authority to develop that.

"The third thing is something the international community has to do, and that is to ask and demand of the Palestinians to develop institutions of law and order, some judicial institutions, [and] financial probity. This has to be done. Otherwise, if you just have an economic growth, that money will flow back to terror soon enough. So you've got to build foundations for society. And what we say is we give security to the Israelis and the Palestinians...We don't give (but this is the process we advocate) to the Palestinian, and then we can proceed through this corridor to political negotiations. If we just promise [peace], as a 'shelf agreement'...it doesn't work that way. [It's like going to a supermarket and buying on the shelf something called peace.] It just doesn't work that way because, in fact, you'll be signaling to Hamas and the other militant Islamic radicals that Israel is already leaving, and now it's just a question of brooming [us,] brushing [us] out quickly, and you do it with terror. So the opposite result will happen.

"[What I'm suggesting] is putting the horse before the cart and not the cart before the horse. I think we've had enough experience now to know what works and what doesn't work. And, we've seen economic peace work elsewhere. We've seen it work in a different context—in Ireland. I'm not sure that it's not working in Cyprus, even though these are huge problems. But what you see is that prosperity breeds a partial agreement, which then breeds more prosperity, which then breeds additional agreements, or at least the possibility to tone down the acerbity of the conflict and also create hope...

"If you build thousands of jobs...in the Palestinian Authority...and people bring food to the table, their wages [will rise, and their investments will be done.] Believe me—that is worth a thousand international conferences and a thousand shelf agreements. So, that's what we would do. We think that the way to prevent the spread of additional bases is to develop bottom-up development of security and prosperity as a prelude to political negotiations."

## Why Has Ahmadinejad Developed More Than Six Thousand Centrifuges in Iran?

"I think [there] is widespread agreement among the leading intelligence agencies of the...Western world, at least—I'm not sure if I would limit it to the Western world—that Iran is...galloping to develop nuclear programs. Now...Ahmadinejad [yesterday or] a few days ago went on a grand tour celebrating another six thousand centrifuges. What is he developing? What does he have those centrifuges for? When they're building ballistic missiles...it's not to carry cement, or medicine. It has only one use. When Iran has the second largest or third largest oil reserves in the world, you know that their energy problem is not uppermost in their mind. Right? So, if it looks like a nuclear program, and it smells like a nuclear program, and it walks like a nuclear program, it's not a duck—it's a nuclear program!

"There was a head of steam being developed in the security council. It was good. It was important. It was real pressure...on the Iranian regime. And, yes, some of it was relaxed after the NIE [National Intelligence Estimate] report. And I think as people now...see that it's the same program, [they'll know] as Ahmadinejad celebrates 'nuclear day'... he's not celebrating nuclear peace. You know exactly what [he's] talking about. And I think the rest of the world is coming back to concrete realization of this problem.

"I don't think that...what we should do in the advent of the development of Iran's nuclear capacity is [to discuss] it publicly. I don't think that's particularly wise. I think what is wise and needed is to make sure that we don't get to that point."

## The Issue of Israel's Safety Is Utmost in Our Minds

"The issue of Israel's safety is one that is uppermost in our minds, and I think of our American friends and many other of our friends in the world. But this is not the only issue—it's merely the first stop.

"You asked me to compare another enemy of the Jewish people—[a sworn] and declared enemy of the Jewish people. Yeah, it began with an attack on the Jews in the late thirties but it didn't end there. And, yes, we paid a terrible price...we don't intend to ever pay again. But we were the first stop. And you know what happened to the world and...other parts of humanity when a very violent creed with messianic conceptions and no inhibition on power [or] moral restraints in the use of weapons came onto the world scene. And in many ways, there is something there as well.

"So I think this is...where the difference lies: There are always differences—historical analogies always suffer the ability to pick at them and find differences—but there is one significant challenge...Am I concerned about the safety and security of my own country? Yes. But, I'm convinced this is a much larger problem—and a much larger threat."

## Will Other Arab Countries in the Middle East Try to Produce Nuclear Weapons?

"Well, there are two possible responses [other Arab countries could have] to the Iranian race to acquire nuclear weapons. One is that... those Arab governments [will] begin to tilt towards Iran out of self-preservation. They'll try to cut deals with them. It just has to do with self-preservation—nothing more than that. And the other [possible response] would be that some of them will try undoubtedly to engage in a nuclear arms race of their own. And...they might be able to do both simultaneously. That could happen too. But either way, it's bad. Now, you know, if the Middle East turns into a nuclear powder keg, that's very, very bad. And…we really don't want that happening in our world. So again, I think that the imperative is clear."

## The Iranian Regime's Strategy

"You asked me about comparisons with Hitler. Well, let me…give you one comparison. There are obviously differences. One is advancing the supremacy of race—the other is advancing the supremacy of creed. [They're] different societies—different histories. But the use of unbridled power [to physically eliminate] enemies…takes place all the time…I'm not sure the world press is fully aware of what is happening inside Iran and how enemies are simply being dispatched. [By] simply being dispatched, I mean, 'killed—murdered.' All the time and publicly too. Publicly and not only quietly. This is taking place all the time in Iran. [It's] a small sect imposing its will with violent means on the society at large, and [it is doing so] for the purpose of outward aggression. There are these similarities…

"The *dissimilarity* is that whereas in the previous case…[the German] regime embarked on a global conflict before developing nuclear weapons, this regime is first developing nuclear weapons before it embarks on a global conflict. And so far…it's giving vent to its aggression by using proxies like Hamas or Hezbollah…and so on. But it is first putting all its efforts in the production of nuclear weapons. And the emphasis is on the word *first*. So there is a difference, and I think it would make you judge which is ultimately more dangerous."

# INTERVIEW TRANSCRIPTS FEATURING RETIRED U.S. LIEUTENANT GENERAL JERRY BOYKIN

The following is an excerpt from a full-length exclusive interview personally conducted by Dr. John Ankerberg and Dr. Jimmy DeYoung in April 2008 in Jerusalem, in which Boykin assessed the threats of surrounding nations to the nation of Israel.

*Ankerberg:* We're sitting here in Jerusalem looking over the Dome of the Rock, and we're talking with retired Lieutenant General Jerry Boykin. And General, I'd like you to tell us a little bit about your service record and your experience.

*Boykin:* Thank you. I graduated from Virginia Tech in 1970 [and] came in the army through the ROTC program. I was commissioned initially as an infantry man. I served some tours in various places, [including] a short period in Vietnam as a young officer. And then I went into special operations, and I spent most of my career in special operations. I first saw real action as we attempted to rescue fifty-three Americans in Tehran in 1980. As you know, that mission was a failure. My next action was...in Grenada, where we liberated the island and rescued one thousand American medical students.

*Ankerberg:* That's where you got wounded, too, didn't you?

*Boykin:* I was wounded there, yes. I got shot with a fifty-caliber. Took a round in the side of the chest and up through the shoulder. But thanks to God's mercy, I completely recovered from that and can still swing a golf club.

*DeYoung:* That's important!

*Boykin:* I'm very happy about that. I also was part of the operations in Panama to liberate the people [there] and turn [the country] back over to the elected government.... I was part of the operation that has come to be known as Black Hawk Down in Mogadishu, Somalia in 1993. And then later I served in the Balkans. And I finished my time in the army as...deputy undersecretary of defense for intelligence. I retired last summer in August.

*Ankerberg:* I want to talk about your experience as we evaluate the different countries of the world and the situation that we're facing right now. First of all, here we are in Israel, and as we've talked to members of the Knesset and other academic people here—professors, people in the military—they all admit that Iran is their number one threat. From the American side, when you were in intelligence, how did you evaluate Iran, and what are we facing right now? What is Israel facing?

*Boykin:* Well, I agree with those Israelis who have told you they fear Iran as their number one threat. I think that it is. I think Iran is the number one threat probably to the whole world. A lot of people don't take Ahmadinejad seriously. But all you have to do is study his background a little bit and you realize that this guy has been a zealot—a fanatic—since he was a very young child. He truly believes that it is his personal responsibility to usher in the *Mahdi* (or the Islamic Messiah). And if you go back and look at some of the early writing, you will find that many like Ahmadinejad believe that that has to occur in a period of chaos and bloodshed for the *Mahdi* to return. Many of them also believe that the caliphate has to be re-established.

Ahmadinejad believes that…he has been called by…Allah…to create…chaos and that bloodshed to bring the *Mahdi* to [the] earth. Given that theology, combined with the fact that he began a number of years ago to develop a nuclear capability and just yesterday he announced that he now has over six thousand centrifuges, which is probably double what he needs for peaceful purposes. And the fact that he believes that if he could destroy Israel in obedience to Allah, even if it meant a retaliatory strike by the Israelis that killed millions of Iranians—he is very comfortable with that. Because Jews and Israel are the infidels. And his people are all followers of Allah. They go to heaven.

*Ankerberg:* How would you rank Iran militarily in the world?

*Boykin:* I'm not sure I can give you a good answer to their military ranking because there are a number of factors there, but I would say that they have a strong military. They learned a lot in the eighties in their war with Iraq. And so they have a very capable military. And I would say that certainly within the Middle East they have one of the strongest militaries… Israel is number one.

*Ankerberg:* How would you evaluate what they are doing via proxy groups and who are they connected with? Who are they supporting?

*Boykin:* Iran has clearly established linkages to Hezbollah. I think that what you will find [in] the summer of 2006…that Iran orchestrated the two-front attack on Israel. Iran supported both Hamas and Hezbollah. Iran is arming Hezbollah in south Lebanon. Iran even paid the families of people in Lebanon who lost family members during the 2006 conflict there. So Iran is very tied to the terrorist groups there. And I think that's…well established. That support continues. It hasn't ceased. And Iran will continue to use Hezbollah and any other terrorist organization that will align themselves with Iran…

*Ankerberg:* What's the military threat from Iran to the United States?

*Boykin:* Well, I think the immediate threat is what Iran is doing in

Iraq by training Shiite insurgents [and arming them, as well as] sending Quds force members over into Iraq to try and kill Americans and other coalition forces. The immediate threat is right there in Iraq. The long-term threat in my view is clearly the nuclear problem. And [our] national intelligence estimate…says that Iran ceased its nuclear program in about 2003. The problem is, you have to read the whole report. And the whole report goes on to say, "But they are capable of fairly rapidly producing nuclear weapons." His own announcement that he had over six thousand centrifuges should be an indicator that he does not have peaceful designs on his nuclear program.

*Ankerberg:* How would you analyze what's going on in Syria, and where do they rank militarily?

*Boykin:* Well, the Syrians…have a capable military. It's certainly not as strong as Iran's…Syria has continued to give safe haven and support to the Hezbollah. Syria also has continued to be a problem for the U.S. and the coalition forces in Iraq because a lot of the foreign fighters have come across the border out of Syria. There has been a steady flow of foreign fighters from many different countries coming into Iraq to get involved in the big jihad there. So Syria has not closed down its borders, and it continues to be problematic.

*Ankerberg:* Go one step further. We're facing an Israeli-Palestinian conflict, and of course, Tony Blair, the Europeans, the United Nations, United States, Condoleezza Rice [are] all trying to put together a peace arrangement. As we've talked with leaders, you've got a stonewall on [both sides.] In terms of the conflict, militarily, how would you describe what is [happening] to Israel right now from the fronts that they're facing?

*Boykin:* Well, I think that Israel has to stay focused on south Lebanon. I think Hezbollah is rebuilding [and] planning. I think it's only a matter of time until there will be another attack out of south Lebanon.[15] Again, [this is] supported by the Syrian[s] as well as the Iranians. I also think that Assad, the president of Syria, has continued [to pursue] his father's desire to have the Golan Heights back. That was lost to the Israelis. It has become a personal thing with Assad, and I think he wants the Golan back. And that will always be problematic in terms of a reason for Syria to attack Israel.

*Ankerberg:* As coalitions are being formed in the Middle East…how would you put together different coalitions that are taking place both in the news as well as what you've learned in intelligence?

*Boykin:* John, I think we have to look at the Middle East and [ask,] "How many countries have actually signed an agreement or a treaty with Israel?" Egypt and Jordan. What about all the rest, particularly those that declare themselves to be Islamic republics? I think that the others either directly or through surrogates are and will probably always be a threat to Israel. The amount of money that comes out of places like Saudi Arabia, for example, that goes to terrorist groups with the stated goal and intention of destroying Israel is a real threat to this country.

*Ankerberg:* How do you see what's happening in Sudan playing into all of this?

*Boykin:* John, there was a period of time where Osama bin Laden himself took refuge in Sudan. He operated…planned…trained, [and] recruited there. And even though he left there, and ultimately went into Afghanistan, he left behind a lot of followers…. Sudan has become an Islamic republic. Sudan continues to support the jihadist cause in many ways. And I think Sudan is a real threat to democracy, as well as to Israel.

*Ankerberg:* [Putin, the former president] of Russia has been involved in many of these countries, [such as] Sudan…Iran…Syria, [and] others. What's his activity all about?

*Boykin:* That's a good question. You know, I think…we're going to see the next czar in Russia. I mean, many experts would tell you he is the most powerful ruler of Russia in the last one hundred years. What are his objectives? Well, I think they're multiple: [First,] I think that he needs warm water ports. He needs to move the large reserves of oil. He needs pipelines. And he needs allies in the Middle East and the gulf. And I think that's what he's working towards.

*Ankerberg:* How do you see what's happening in Libya? You know, we have taken the...sanctions off of Libya because Qaddafi has basically said that he's going to let our military analysts like yourself in there to examine everything. How do you evaluate Qaddafi right now in Libya?

*Boykin:* I've very suspicious of Qaddafi. I think that Qaddafi [and] these overtures of peace and reconciliation need to be watched very carefully. I'm not convinced that Qaddafi is the leopard that has changed his [spots,] so I think we need to watch [him] very carefully. I think there's enough evidence [of] a history of terrorist activity there [to keep us from assuming] that those terrorist activities have ceased [and], that those who [support jihad and radical Islam] have disappeared. I think they're still there. I think they still have influence. I think they're still planning attacks and nefarious things against Israel...the United States, and other Western democracies.

*Ankerberg:* NATO has a base in Turkey, and we've been close friends with [the government of] Turkey, and they've applied for membership in the EU (the European Union). At the same time, the EU has kind of backed away from that. And there's another faction that's coming up in Turkey. How do you evaluate them and the importance of Turkey to the Middle East?

*Boykin:* Well, I think Turkey is strategic, and...this is one of the really difficult issues for NATO. Because on the one hand, we have a NATO alliance, and Turkey has always been a member of that. On the other hand, we have the European Union arising and countries like Germany have refused to allow Turkey to join the European Union. The fear is that [this]...is then driving them towards the Islamic camp to where they become, rather than the secular state that they have been for decades, they become an Islamic republic, which would fracture NATO [and] create another problem in the Middle East. [It would probably throw the balance of power] in the Middle East way out of kilter.

*Ankerberg:* Part of your official job was to analyze counterterrorism… How do we counter some of the stuff that we see going on in the world? How in the world can we protect against the supply of oil being cut off from the Middle East? And if it was [cut off, preventing oil supply to America and the rest of the world,] what kind of crisis are we looking at?

*Boykin:* I think [when] we look beyond the Middle East, [we] realize the crisis is actually larger than the way you've described it. We get oil from Venezuela [and] Nigeria, both of which have major problems… Both could cut off our oil at any time. Very soon we will import about sixty percent of our oil requirements…That's fifty-eight to sixty percent of the known reserves in the world today. And we're dependent upon that. I think we have a huge problem.

Now, the gulf countries have continued that supply of oil. But the fact of the matter is, they could cut it off. Or they could jack the prices up so high that it would destroy our economy. I recently read a book by John Walvoord and Mark Hitchcock—*Armageddon, Oil, and Terror*—and I think it describes what you've just talked about very well in terms of the problems that America could face as a result of either an increase of prices or a lack of oil.

*DeYoung:* General, we've been watching as China has been taking control of [many resources worldwide.] Where do you see China in the geopolitical activities of the future? Is it a superpower militarily? Is that yet to come? Give us an evaluation of [their consumption of oil.]

*Boykin:* You know, I saw some assessments recently that [made me] think in about the next twenty years, China will consume more oil than all the nations in the world today. So if you look at the growing appetite for energy in China…then you have to assess that China is going to be competing—certainly with the United States—but also with the whole world for a limited amount of oil in the future. Now, what does that mean to us? It probably means that the price of oil is going to go up astronomically. And our economy is just simply going to have to figure out how to deal with that. Or we're going to have to start producing more oil within our own country, [which is] a very difficult decision for our policymakers. We haven't built a refinery since about 1976. We have refused to drill up in Anwar and in other parts of the gulf regions and so forth. So the U.S. is coming to a crisis, and China is very much at the heart of that because it will continue to consume huge amounts of oil.

China's all over Africa [and the Chinese] are investing in Africa in very large ways...The Chinese are also in South and Central America... For example, they're making huge investments [in Panama]. I think the United States needs to take a very serious look at what the Chinese are doing and make some assessments in terms of U.S. policy.

# Experts Interviewed for *Israel Under Fire*

All interviews took place in Israel during April 2008.

1. Major General (retired) Jacob Amidror, the former head of Israeli Defense Force Intelligence

2. Mr. Moshi Arens, the three-time minister of defense and ambassador to the U.S. for Israel

3. Dr. Gabriel Barkay, PhD—archaeologist and Professor of Land of Israel Studies, Bar-Ilan University

4. Dr. Alexander Bligh, the professor and chairman of Department of Israel and Middle East Politics at the Ariel University Center

5. Dr. Megan Broshi, former curator of the Israel Museum and Shrine of the Book

6. Lieut. Gen. (retired) William G. "Jerry" Boykin—U.S. deputy undersecretary of defense for intelligence

7. Daniel "Dan" Dayan, the chairman of the Yeshua Council; The Jewish Communities of Judea, Samaria, and Gush Katif

8. Meir Ben-Dov, an Israeli archaeologist and professor

9. Isaac Dror, the director of education programs and of Independence Hall Museum—also an expert on modern Israeli history

10. Mr. Benjamin Elon, a member of the Israeli Knesset

11. Micah and Shoshanna Harrari, owners of the Harp Factory in Jerusalem, Israel

12. Adnan Husseini, the presidential adviser on Jerusalem of the Palestine Liberation Organization

13. Itamar Marcus, the director of the Palestinian Media Watch in Jerusalem, Israel

14. Israel Medad, a resident of Shiloh, Samaria

15. Benjamin Netanyahu, the prime minister of Israel[*]

16. Abraham Rabinovich, an Israeli journalist and author

17. Reuven (Ruby) Rivlin, the Speaker of the Knesset (the third-highest ranking position in Israel)

18. Gershon Salomon, the founder and director of Temple Mount Faithful

19. Dr. Hillel Weiss, the spokesperson for the modern-day Sanhedrin

20. David Wilder, the spokesperson for the Jewish community in Hebron

---

[*] Special thanks goes to The Israel Project for giving us permission to use Benjamin Netanyahu's press converence material.

# NOTES

1. See our interview with Itzik Dror.
2. Larry Collins and Dominique Lapierre, *O Jerusalem!* (New York: Simon & Schuster, 1972), pp. 163-65.
3. See Appendix A for the complete transcript of this interview.
4. April 2008.
5. See http://abcnews.go.com/Politics/US/Story?id=5281043&page=1.
6. See http://web.israelinsider.com/Articles/Security/12785.htm.
7. See http://www.nydailynews.com/news/us_world/2008/06/06/2008-06-06_minister_israel_will_attack_iran_if_it_d.html.
8. See http://www.tbshamden.com/index.php?option=com_content&task=view&id=224&Itemid=51.
9. Ibid.
10. Roy B. Zuck and Donald Campbell, *Basic Bible Interpretation* (Colorado Springs, CO: David C. Cook, 2002), p. 29.
11. Quoted from the transcript of "The Great Debate on the Book of Revelation," ATRI Publications, 2008. Available at *www.johnankerberg.org*.
12. As cited by John Walvoord on this verse in *The Bible Knowledge Commentary* (Colorado Springs, CO: David C. Cook Publishing, 1983).
13. This chapter adapted from John Ankerberg and Dillon Burroughs, *Middle East Meltdown: Oil, Israel, and the Religion Behind the Crisis* (Eugene, OR: Harvest House, 2007), pp. 171-76.
14. John F. Walvoord, *Armageddon, Oil and the Middle East Crisis,* rev. ed. (Grand Rapids, MI: Zondervan, 1990), pp. 227-28.
15. Boykin's prediction on this issue has already been fulfilled as of January 2009.

*The Peace Vista on the Golan Heights*

Left to right (seated): Alan Weathers and Rob Curschman

Left to right (first row): Jeff Pohorski, Jimmy DeYoung, Jr., Darlene Ankerberg, and Judy DeYoung

Left to right (second row): Rob Whitehurst, Jimmy DeYoung, Sr., John Ankerberg, and David Nixon

Left to right (back row): Gal Rei-Koren

*Filming the Mount of Olives and the Kidron Valley*

Left to right: Rob Curschman and Jimmy DeYoung

## About the Authors

**DR. JOHN ANKERBERG** is host of the award-winning TV and radio program *The John Ankerberg Show,* seen in all 50 states and 200 countries. Author of nearly 90 books, his research is used by universities and experts worldwide on world religion and the evidence for Christianity. He has three earned degrees: a Master of Arts in church history and the philosophy of Christian thought, a Master of Divinity from Trinity Evangelical Divinity School, and a Doctor of Ministry from Luther Rice Seminary. John lives with his wife, Darlene, and daughter, Michelle, in Chattanooga, Tennessee.

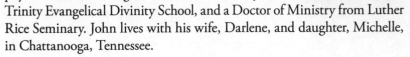

══════════════ **johnankerberg.org** ══════════════

**DR. JIMMY DEYOUNG** is the president of Prophecy Today and a frequent television host for Day of Discovery. His radio reports are heard worldwide on over 1500 outlets. A journalist who has lived in Israel since 1991, DeYoung has interviewed several Israeli prime ministers, government leaders, and diplomats of Middle Eastern nations. A noted conference speaker, Dr. DeYoung is a graduate of Tennessee Temple and holds a PhD in prophecy from Louisiana Baptist University.

══════════════ **prophecytoday.com** ══════════════

**DILLON BURROUGHS** is a writer on issues of faith and culture and has collaborated on several books with John Ankerberg. Dillon lives with his wife, Deborah, and three children in Tennessee.

══════════════ **readdb.com** ══════════════

# ISRAEL UNDER FIRE DVD

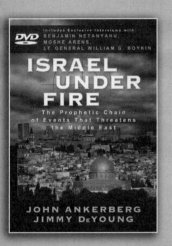

In 120 eye-opening minutes, apologist John Ankerberg and journalist Jimmy DeYoung document for you many signs that point—*right now*—toward apocalyptic conflict in the Middle East, including explosive issues such as

- preparations for rebuilding the Jewish temple on one of Islam's most holy places
- external and internal threats to Israel from Palestinian Arabs
- Iran's nuclear capability and intention to "wipe Israel off the map"

You'll also witness incisive interviews with figures such as Israeli politicians Benjamin Netanyahu and Moshi Arens and Palestinian Authority spokesman Adnan Husseini. Conversations with numerous rabbis, religious leaders, and other guests round out some of the most exclusive interview footage on current Middle East spiritual–political issues.

As a terrific companion to the book, the *Israel Under Fire DVD* offers viewers unmatched insight into the events now being generated by peoples, alliances, and religions—events that will unavoidably involve North Americans and the other billions of the globe.

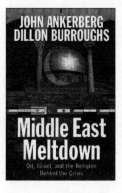

### MIDDLE EAST MELTDOWN

The news headlines from the war-torn Middle East are constantly changing, and though those countries are on the opposite side of the globe, the events unfolding there have a powerful effect on America. But the complexity of all that's happening makes it difficult to understand what it means and how it affects us. Authors John Ankerberg and Dillon Burroughs help bring clarity to the issues as they answer these important questions:

- Why does peace continue to elude the Arab nations and Israel?
- What part does Middle East oil have in all this?
- Where do Iran, Lebanon, and Hezbollah fit into the big picture?
- What can we expect from today's new breed of terrorists?
- What does the United States have at stake?

Readers who have perceived the Middle East conflict as too complicated to understand will gain a new appreciation for how today's events fits into God's plan for the future.

### THE FACTS ON ISLAM

John Ankerberg, John Weldon, and Dillon Burroughs team up to revise and update *The Facts on Islam,* a popular Facts On book (more than 1.9 million copies of books from this series sold). Known for their extensive research and Bible knowledge, these authors offer readers the essential facts they need to evaluate and discuss today's issues regarding Islam.

Whether readers are merely curious or searching for specific information, *The Facts on Islam* will give them what they are looking for—easy–to–understand, factual, and relevant information about Islam.